Heidegger and th
Roots of Existential Therapy

Other titles in the School of Psychotherapy and Counselling (SPC) Series of Regent's College

General Editor: Ernesto Spinelli

Embodied Theories Sue Marshall and Ernesto Spinelli
Heart of Listening Rosalind Pearmain
Wise Therapy: Philosophy for Counsellors Tim Le Bon

SPC SERIES

Heidegger and the Roots of Existential Therapy

Hans W. Cohn

continuum
LONDON • NEW YORK

CONTINUUM
The Tower Building, 11 York Road, London SE1 7NX
370 Lexington Avenue, New York NY 10017-6503

www.continuumbooks.com

First published 2002

British Library Cataloguing-in-Publication Data
A catalogue record for this book is available from the British Library.

ISBN: 0-8264-5573-5 (hardback)
0-8264-5509-3 (paperback)

Typeset by Kenneth Burnley, Wirral, Cheshire
Printed and bound in Great Britain by Lightning Source.

In memory of Udi

Contents

Series Editor's Introduction

IT IS BOTH A GREAT HONOUR AND A PLEASURE to welcome readers to the SPC Series.

The School of Psychotherapy and Counselling at Regent's College (SPC) is one of the largest and most widely respected psychotherapy, counselling and counselling psychology training institutes in the UK. The SPC Series published by Continuum marks a major development in the School's mission to initiate and develop novel perspectives centred upon the major topics of debate within the therapeutic professions so that their impact and influence upon the wider social community may be more adequately understood and assessed.

A brief overview of SPC

Although its origins lie in an innovative study programme developed by Antioch University, USA, in 1977, SPC has been in existence in its current form since 1990. SPC's MA in Psychotherapy and Counselling programme obtained British validation with City University in 1991. More recently, the MA in Existential Counselling Psychology obtained accreditation from the British Psychological Society. SPC was also the first UK institute to develop a research-based MPhil/PhD programme in Psychotherapy and Counselling, and this has been validated by City University since 1992. Largely on the impetus of its first Dean, Emmy van Deurzen, SPC became a full training and accrediting member of the United Kingdom Council for Psychotherapy (UKCP) and continues to maintain a strong and active presence in that organization through its Professional Members, many of whom also hold professional affiliations with the British Psychological Society (BPS), the British Association of Counselling and Psychotherapy (BACP), the Society for Existential Analysis (SEA) and the European Society for Communicative Psychotherapy (ESCP).

SPC's other programmes include: a Foundation Certificate in Psychotherapy and Counselling, Advanced Professional Diploma Programmes in Existential Psychotherapy and Integrative Psychotherapy, and a series of intensive Continuing Professional Development and related adjunct courses such as its innovative Legal and Family Mediation Programmes.

With the personal support of the President of Regent's College, Mrs Gillian Payne, SPC has recently established the Psychotherapy and Counselling Consultation Centre housed on the college campus which provides individual and group therapy for both private individuals and organizations.

As a unique centre for learning and professional training, SPC has consistently emphasized the comparative study of psychotherapeutic theories and techniques while paying careful and accurate attention to the philosophical assumptions underlying the theories being considered and the philosophical coherence of those theories to their practice-based standards and professional applications within a diversity of private and public settings. In particular, SPC fosters the development of faculty and graduates who think independently, are theoretically well informed and are able skilfully and ethically to apply the methods of psychotherapy and counselling in practice, in the belief that knowledge advances through criticism and debate, rather than by uncritical adherence to received wisdom.

The integrative attitude of SPC

The underlying ethos upon which the whole of SPC's educational and training programme rests is its *integrative attitude*, which can be summarized as follows.

There exists a multitude of perspectives in current psychotherapeutic thought and practice, each of which expresses a particular philosophical viewpoint on an aspect of being human. No one single perspective or set of underlying values and assumptions is universally shared.

Given that a singular, or shared, view does not exist, SPC seeks to enable a learning environment which allows competing and diverse models to be considered both conceptually and experientially so that their areas of interface and divergence can be exposed, considered and clarified. This aim espouses the value of holding the tension between contrasting and often contradictory ideas, of 'playing with' their experiential possibilities and of allowing a paradoxical security which can 'live with' and at times even thrive in the absence of final and fixed truths.

SPC defines this aim as 'the integrative attitude' and has designed all of its courses so that its presence will challenge and stimulate all aspects of our students' and trainees' learning experience. SPC believes that this deliberate engagement with difference should be reflected in the manner in which the faculty relate to students, clients and colleagues at all levels. In such a way this attitude may be seen as the lived expression of the foundational ethos of SPC.

The SPC Series

The series evolved out of a number of highly encouraging and productive discussions between the Publishing Director at Continuum Books, Mr Robin Baird-Smith, and the present Academic Dean of SPC, Professor Ernesto Spinelli.

From the start, it was recognized that SPC, through its faculty and Professional Members, was in a unique position to provide a series of wide-ranging, accessible and pertinent texts intended to challenge, inspire and influence debate in a variety of issues and areas central to therapeutic enquiry. Further, SPC's focus and concern surrounding the ever more pervasive impact of therapeutic ideas and practices upon all sections of contemporary society highlighted the worth, if not necessity, of a series that could address key topics from an informed, critical and non-doctrinal perspective.

The publication of the first three texts in the series during 2001 marks the beginning of what is hoped will be a long and fruitful relationship between SPC and Continuum. More than that, there exists the hope that the series will become identified by professionals and public alike as an invaluable contributor to the advancement of psychotherapy and counselling as a vigorously self-critical, socially minded and humane profession.

PROFESSOR ERNESTO SPINELLI
Series Editor

Foreword

PERHAPS SERENDIPITOUSLY, just before beginning this foreword, I chanced upon a lengthy review of Anthony Gottlieb's *The Dream of Reason*, the first of two volumes dealing with the history of Western philosophy. Although the review is very positive, its final sentence is somewhat critical, if not downright unusual, in that it urges Gottlieb to recant his contention that '[a]ny subject that is responsible for producing Heidegger . . . owes the world an apology'.

What is it about Martin Heidegger that provokes such powerful, and contradictory, reactions? Lauded by many as one of the most brilliant and significant philosophers of the twentieth century, nonetheless it remains evident that, a quarter of a century after his death, he continues to instil a fair degree of unease. No doubt, Heidegger's personal and political association with German National Socialism can, in part, explain this discomfiture. Even so, might it also be the case that what Heidegger sought to convey to us concerning the question of our very existence persists in challenging the most basic of our assumptions regarding what it is to be human?

Hans W. Cohn was already a practising psychotherapist when he began to consider Heidegger's challenge in the light of its potential impact on his own understanding of the fundamental assumptions within the profession and upon his work with clients. The present book is, in many ways, his attempt to present his conclusions on this matter. And what conclusions they are!

I first heard Hans Cohn express some of the ideas discussed in this book in 1989 during one of the initial meetings of the then newly-founded Society for Existential Analysis. I remember being struck, on that occasion, by the ease and clarity with which he conveyed Heidegger's complex ideas. I have heard Hans speak on such matters many times since, both in formal lectures and in informal discussions with him. On all occasions I have walked away from such meetings feeling enriched by them. As his many students will confirm, my experience is by no means unique. It is, therefore, both a great pleasure and no less an honour for me, as General Editor of the SPC Series, to be associated with the publication of *Heidegger and the Roots of Existential Therapy*.

As readers will learn, Heidegger was himself interested in the issues raised and dilemmas provoked by psychotherapy. For many years, through his friendship with Medard Boss, the founder of the approach to psychotherapy known as *Daseinsanalysis,* Heidegger lectured to trainee and professional psychotherapists, focusing upon the interface between his philosophical arguments and therapeutic practice. Cohn clarifies and comments upon many of the points raised in these lectures throughout his book. This, in itself, imbues his text with unique value since, as yet, the notes taken during these lectures have not been published in an English translation. This is, Cohn tells us, a great pity since in many ways they provide one of the most accessible and straightforward entry points to many of Heidegger's key ideas.

But Cohn provides his readers with much besides useful clarificatory commentary. He suggests that there exist many more pertinent and disturbing challenges for psychotherapy to be derived from the reading and consideration of Heidegger's arguments. This, for me, is the heart of Hans Cohn's book. And in its aim, its clarity of language and succinct explication of the issues being raised it stands alone; I know of no other book like it. Although no longer identifying himself as a poet (three collections of his works were published some years ago, and a new collection was published in 1999), Hans Cohn brings a poetic sensitivity and unsparing concision to his discussion. And, as with the finest examples of creative endeavour, readers will be rewarded with novel nuances of meaning and understanding each time they return to read his words anew.

All students of Heidegger, be they philosophers or psychotherapists, will find a great deal to stimulate and surprise them in *Heidegger and the Roots of Existential Therapy.* And, as well, they may find that, notwithstanding any required apologies, both fields of inquiry have much to benefit from the critical consideration of Heidegger's challenge to them. In this, too, Hans Cohn has provided a way.

PROFESSOR ERNESTO SPINELLI

References

Burnyeat, M. F. (2001) 'Philosophy for winners', *The New York Review of Books,* 48 (17): 55–7.

Cohn, H. W. (1999) *With All Five Senses.* London: Menard Press.

Gottlieb, A. (2001) *The Dream of Reason: a History of Western Philosophy from the Greeks to the Renaissance.* New York: Norton.

Introduction

IT SEEMS IMPORTANT TO ME to make clear at the very beginning what this book is trying to do. It is not offering another exposition of Martin Heidegger's philosophical thought – there are already many of these, some of them excellent, and there will be many more as new volumes of his collected works are being published and, I hope, translated. I am not a professional philosopher but a psychotherapist with a long experience of trying to understand people's difficulties, including my own.

Over many years I felt the need to change the conceptual framework within which I was doing my work. My original psychoanalytical orientation, with its reliance on hypothetical intrapsychic processes, increasingly failed to help me with my attempts to grasp the actual experiences I had with my clients and with myself.

In my search for other points of view I came upon the writings of some Swiss therapists. These therapists were strongly influenced by the philosophy of Martin Heidegger and eventually created a new theoretical foundation for the practice of psychotherapy, which they called 'Daseinsanalyse', that is 'the analysis of being there'. Some aspects of their approach answered my own questions and I moved gradually from a psychoanalytic to an existential-phenomenological understanding of our life as human beings. Existential phenomenology is, as I see it, basically the creation of Martin Heidegger, rooted in the insights of Edmund Husserl.

This was not a question of 'applying' Heidegger's existential concepts to the practice of psychotherapy – rather it was the realization that some of his understanding of the way human beings exist reflected my own and therefore underlies my therapeutic practice. As this understanding is basically different from a psychodynamic approach, it is not surprising that I felt confused and out of tune with the theoretical assumptions of the latter. Further study of Heidegger's thinking deepened this experience.

Martin Heidegger is, of course, known as one of the important philosophers of existence – he refused to be called an 'existentialist' – and his influence on contemporary philosophy is admitted to be considerable. This is despite certain reservations about some of the more radical aspects of his thinking, and the almost universal condemnation of his comparatively short-lived, but nevertheless deeply shocking, political alliance with the Nazis. My own response to this involvement will be included in this book.

But no matter how well known Heidegger may be as a philosopher, his impact on psychotherapy has been strangely neglected, particularly in English-speaking countries. We have a number of books illustrating the relevance of Heidegger's ideas on art, language, politics and ethics. We have some biographies. We have explorations of East Asian influences on his thinking. But nobody has yet looked in any depth at his importance for psychotherapy, or his involvement with it. This is the aim of this book.

I have already mentioned Heidegger's influence on a group of Swiss therapists and their creation of 'Daseinsanalyse'. As far as I know this was the first attempt to develop a method of psychotherapy from 'existential' roots. In addition, Heidegger was personally and actively involved in this approach by teaching – from 1959 to 1969 – psychotherapists and psychiatrists an outline of his world-view and its potential relevance to their work. There will be a more detailed account of this in later chapters.

Under the influence of an increasing interest in aspects of existential philosophy, different groups of therapists in different countries, seeking an alternative to therapies rooted in psychoanalytic theories, called themselves 'existential', though giving different meanings to this word. Some of them included Heidegger's views, others did not. None, as far as I know, based their approach consistently or predominantly on Heidegger's way of seeing 'existence' as the Swiss School attempted to do.

At this point the question arises: why does this book not lean more closely on the writings of those Swiss therapists who were present, so to speak, at the very birth of the existential orientation in psychotherapy? These were, among others, Medard Boss, who had become a close friend of Heidegger, had invited him to Switzerland and later became the director of the Institute for Daseinsanalysis, and the present head of the Institute, Gion Condrau. The psychiatrist Ludwig Binswanger, who created a 'Daseinsanalyse' of his own which was essentially phenomenologically descriptive and not conceived as a 'therapy', went his own way early on.

An appreciation and critique of the work of these 'Daseinsanalysts', as it is presented in their writings, requires a book of its own. Such a book would be of great importance, as these therapists were pioneers of existential therapy, in direct contact with Heidegger for many years, and their writings are deeply illuminating. Their view of Heidegger's relevance to therapy differs, however, in many ways from my own. Perhaps they were too closely involved with the beginnings of this new development and therefore overemphasized some aspects of it at the expense of others. As far as I know there is not yet a clear and comprehensive overview of this group's relation to Heidegger's thinking, particularly as he expressed it in the *Zollikon Seminars* when he addressed a group of Swiss psychiatrists and therapists. There is certainly not an English version of such an overview.

Indebted though I am to the example and writings of the Swiss School, it is not here my aim to question some of their assumptions or to express my agreement with others. So what is my book trying to do? It is looking at what seems to me the most important aspects of Heidegger's thinking in order to examine their relevance to a therapy which is both 'phenomenological' and 'existential', giving these words the meaning which, in my understanding, Heidegger has given them. My main sources will be *Being and Time* (using the translation by Macquarrie and Robinson, though I shall at times draw on Joan Stambaugh's more recent translation) and Boss's protocols of Heidegger's lectures in Zollikon. In spite of Heidegger's developments in his later thinking, these lectures are, in my view, more closely based on *Being and Time* than we might expect. They also illustrate the much earlier work by concrete examples and observations on themes he had not explored before, as for instance the body/mind problem. (These protocols, published in German, are quoted in my own translation.)

In the end we are left with a wide-reaching context for the pursuit of an existential-phenomenological therapy. It cannot be 'complete' as Heidegger said little about themes, which are crucial for therapists. However, I believe that someone who has understood Heidegger's way of seeing our relation to the world, to others and to ourselves will find possibilities to include in such an understanding those aspects of 'being' which Heidegger has not explicitly talked about. As we shall see, existential thinking is always 'open' and can therefore never be complete.

Acknowledgements

THIS BOOK IS DEDICATED to the memory of my friend Udi Eichler with whom I discussed many of the issues that are addressed in it. He knew before his death that I was going to write it and that it would be dedicated to him. I think of him often.

The book is based on a series of seminars about Martin Heidegger's impact on existential therapy given to students of the Advanced Diploma in Existential Psychotherapy at the School of Psychotherapy and Counselling, Regent's College, London. I thank the present Dean, Professor Ernesto Spinelli, for actively helping this book to see the light of day. I also thank Lucia Moja-Strasser, the director of the Advanced Diploma Course, for initiating these seminars and asking me to give them for a number of years, as well as for her continuous appreciation and encouragement. My students I thank for their questions which prevented me from giving any final answers.

I thank Sarah Young for her generous help, once again combining her technical skill in preparing the manuscript with her professional knowledge of its themes and the questions it raises.

And I thank my friend Jenny H. Steward for her great openness and engaged response to what I attempt to say which, time and again, has helped me to face and overcome my doubts.

Note on the Translation of the *Zollikon Seminars*

AT THE TIME OF MY WRITING THIS BOOK, no English translation of Heidegger's *Zollikon Seminars* had appeared.

There is now an English translation avaliable as *Zollikon Seminars* by Martin Heidegger (edited by Medard Boss), translated by Franz K. Mayr and Richard R. Askay, and published by Northwestern University Press.

As stated in the Introduction, all translations from the German of the *Zollikon Seminars* are my own.

HANS W. COHN
London, 2002

1 | Why Heidegger?

The question

For many existential therapists the question 'Why Heidegger?' may seem unexpected. They tend to take it for granted that Heidegger is an important existential thinker, his name appears in all books on existential philosophy and therapy, at least as the author of *Being and Time* (1962). A reference to some of his ideas, such as 'Being-in-the-world' and 'Being-towards-Death' can frequently be found. And still it often seems to me as if many existential therapists – or therapists who see themselves as 'existential' – show a certain reluctance to engage themselves with Heidegger and they betray an unexpressed wish to have an existential therapy without him. A feeling comes across that Heidegger's place in existential thinking is a burden and an embarrassment.

Some writers express these feelings comparatively openly. There are, essentially, two problem areas that give rise to open criticism – one is Heidegger's language and the other is his political behaviour. These problem areas, I think, need to be faced, and they may well underlie the reluctance of writers and practitioners to engage themselves more fully with Heidegger's thinking. Therefore, I propose to look first of all briefly at those aspects that most frequently appear in open critical discussions: Heidegger's style and his involvement with the Nazis.

Obstacles

The fact that Heidegger does not write in English is, of course, an obstacle. But many German readers also have difficulties with his style. At times his writing is close to poetic prose, and he often gives new meaning to familiar words, frequently going back to their origins. Macquarrie and Robinson's translation of *Being and Time* – in some way perhaps his most difficult piece of writing – is of course a formidable, even heroic achievement. But it does not, in my view, succeed in recreating its poetic quality, and some of their translations are inevitably misleading.

It has also been suggested that musical structures could help to understand the movement of Heidegger's thinking. George Pattison proposes the fugue as 'a kind of structure that resists incorporation into any linear progression . . . in which discord and conflict are resolved into a final unity' (Pattison, 2000, p. 23). My own comparison is that with a theme, that is 'Being', and its many variations where the theme's various possibilities are separately worked out. In any case, there is in Heidegger's writings no clear argument leading to a definite conclusion. In spite of its complexity you cannot evade *Being and Time* if you wish to acquaint yourself with the basic structure of Heidegger's thought. He himself returns to his early work towards the end of his life when he is teaching Swiss psychiatrists and students of psychiatry in Zollikon.

The other problem area that frequently opens itself up for discussion is Heidegger's involvement with the Nazis. It is a fact – and a great deal of evidence has been published about it – that Heidegger became a party member and for a comparatively short but significant time was an important figure in German academic life as Rector of Freiburg University. What is worse is that he never expressed publicly any regret about this, nor did he find anything to say about the Holocaust. He admitted that he had been wrong in his assessment and expectations of this political movement but he took no responsibility for his extraordinary mistake.

As a German Jew, who was fortunate enough to escape the fate of six million other Jews and become an existential therapist, I had to face some difficult decisions. Some years back at a conference on Heidegger at the Goethe Institute two possibilities seemed to offer themselves to deal with this dilemma, neither of which I could accept. At this conference, people either minimized Heidegger's political involvement, or they felt it could only lead to a total rejection of his work.

The problem can perhaps be formulated like this: can a person's creative contribution as a thinker (or for that matter as a poet or composer) be taken seriously when there are indisputable reasons to question or reject his or her personal actions? When we believe that a person's 'self' is of one piece and that every aspect of it is necessarily reflected by any other aspect, so that a person questionable in one way will also be questionable in any other way, then Heidegger cannot be acceptable as a thinker.

But though this is an understandable view that reflects our deep desire for harmony and wholeness – it is an idealistic rather than a phenomenological view. As I put it in a previous paper:

> The concept of a balanced independent self is an aspect of a certain psychological tradition and is perhaps a reflection of the Cartesian notion of the subject as a thinking disembodied substance that stands apart from the world and is our only certainty ... It is the idealistic wish for an unconflicted wholeness that, I feel, lives in all of us. However, a phenomenological approach proposes to understand subjects intersubjectively, not unchanging and apart from an ever-changing context. A person is not good or bad, creative or destructive as such, once and for all, but good or bad, creative or destructive within a particular context. (Cohn, 1997b, p. 97)

I do not think that Heidegger's political attitude can or should be defended. At a later point we shall consider its connection with some of his philosophical ideas – and there certainly is such a connection. But this connection, in my view, is not one in which the philosophy validates the behaviour but rather it is one in which the behaviour is a betrayal of the philosophy.

The question is, in the end: are Heidegger's ideas worth thinking about, are they illuminating and helpful? Or more particularly: are they relevant for psychotherapy? This book attempts to answer this question. For I believe that they are.

Shortcuts

Objections to Heidegger's way of writing and to his political activities are concrete issues and, as I said, frequently discussed. The reluctance of some authors to engage themselves more fully with Heidegger's ideas, even if they refer to them, is more elusive. A certain half-heartedness in the use of Heidegger's often quite radical propositions may, in my view, lead to a distortion of meaning and to contradictions. Let me give a few examples to illustrate my point.

1. The important difference between Husserl's concept of phenomenology and Heidegger's modification of it is rarely clarified. Heidegger did not accept Husserl's idea of 'reduction' – he did not think one could or should put the 'world' in brackets. Heidegger's existential phenomenology does not acknowledge Husserl's 'epochē'.
2. Heidegger's specific definition of the word 'existence' is rarely mentioned, and a more colloquial and somewhat woolly usage is, on the whole, preferred.
3. Heidegger's illuminating distinction between the 'ontological' and the 'ontic' is rarely applied.
4. 'Being-in-the-world' is perhaps the most frequently quoted

> Heideggerian concept, but the fact that it goes against the very grain of Western thinking, challenging as it does the Cartesian split between subject and world which in many ways still dominates us, is, in my view, not sufficiently emphasized.

I would like to stress that this is not a question of agreeing with any or all of Heidegger's views. But I think that once you have decided to take his contribution into account at all, there is some need to present it as accurately as possible and when there is disagreement it needs to be stated and argued. My feeling is that some authors think they ought to include Heidegger but really wish to keep him out, and this can only lead to confusion and misunderstanding.

I sometimes wonder whether one of the reasons for this kind of selective use is the wish to integrate the radical position of an existential-phenomenological stance with the more familiar and culturally more acceptable ways of therapy that most psychotherapists have been trained to follow. There may at times be a failure to realize how radically different his view in fact is, and how a proper consideration of this might provide a fundamentally different understanding of therapeutic practice.

Why Heidegger?

This sketchy outline of the various dimensions of our question 'Why Heidegger?' provides us with a framework within which to attempt to answer it. Factually, as we shall see, Heidegger played an active part in contributing to the first model of an existentially orientated psychotherapy. More importantly he is a source and influence, albeit to varying degrees, for most contemporary existential thinkers. In his writings he also offers a contact with two philosophers who are often considered to be forerunners of existential thinking, namely Kierkegaard and Nietzsche.

This does not mean that all existential philosophers are in agreement with Heidegger (or he with them). It does mean, however, that his telling and consequential concepts provide the basis for agreement or disagreement. And we shall see that this is so for psychotherapists too.

2 Heidegger's Way to Psychotherapy

The meaning of Being

The last sentence of Heidegger's inaugural lecture at Freiburg University reads: 'Why are there beings at all, and why not rather nothing?' (Heidegger, 1993, p. 110). Heidegger calls this 'the basic question of metaphysics' and it sums up his own philosophical concern. It is also the question that we tend to forget. We say, of course, that rocks are hard, roses are red, and that human beings are the most intelligent beings on earth. But whatever we say they 'are', we can only say it because they *are,* and what Heidegger stresses in the second part of his sentence is that they might not be – that there might be nothing.

So what is this 'Being' which is the ground of whatever we might say about beings? Heidegger pursued this question throughout his life, but though he said a great deal about Being, the question of what it *is* remained, to some extent, open to the very end. Whether we agree with Heidegger that this is indeed the crucial question or not, we might wonder how it is relevant for the difficulties which human beings bring into what we call 'therapy' to be explored.

There seems, in fact, a great gap between the meaning of 'Being' as such and the meaning of the frustrations and distortions of the individual lives of human beings. If Heidegger pursued the meaning of Being throughout his life without finding a clear answer to this question, how relevant could his thinking be to the many questions which are the fabric of psychotherapy?

This doubt has, of course, been expressed and is *one* of the strands of the half-heartedness with which Heidegger's involvement with the foundations of existential psychotherapy has been greeted by a number of theorists and practitioners. But their doubts might be met, I suggest, if they considered the first step Heidegger takes in the pursuit of Being. He proposes that the beings that need to be asked about Being are those who have an experience of it, and are intimately concerned with it – that is human beings. *Being and Time* is, to a great extent, the analysis of the Being of human beings which Heidegger sees as radically different from the Being of other beings. It is just because human beings can be aware of their Being, and have always already some understanding of it, however vague, that they are also able to forget it. This is hardly true of rocks and roses.

Dasein

To emphasize this special way of being, Heidegger does what he often does – he uses familiar words in a new way. He does not speak of 'human beings' but of 'Dasein', and Dasein's way of being he calls 'existence'.

The German word 'Dasein' is quite commonly used and is translated as 'presence' and 'existence'. It does not necessarily apply to human beings alone. Heidegger, in using it to characterize *human* beings, pays attention, as he frequently does, to the literal meaning of the word: this is '*there*-being' or as we usually say 'being there'.

Heidegger's emphasis on *there* does not refer to a location in space – a rock has this too. Rather Heidegger's 'there' is that place of openness in which we encounter other beings as well as our own involvement with the world. In a later development of Heidegger's thinking, this 'there' becomes the place where Being appears, it becomes the 'there of Being'.

What I am trying to stress is the centrality of human beings and their relation to Being in Heidegger's exploration of his 'crucial question', and that the question could not even be asked without 'Dasein' to ask it – a 'Dasein' that is concerned with Being.

In *Being and Time*, Heidegger introduces 'Dasein' to us in the following way:

> Dasein is an entity, which does not just occur among other entities. Rather it is ... distinguished by the fact that, in its very Being, that Being is an *issue* for it ... this implies that Dasein, in its Being, has a relationship towards that Being ... And this means further that there is some way in which Dasein understands itself in its Being, and that to some degree it does so explicitly ... *Understanding of Being is itself a definite characteristic of Dasein's Being.* (Heidegger, 1962, p. 32; emphasis in the original)

Existence

This leads to Heidegger's introduction of his specific use of the word 'existence': 'The kind of Being towards which Dasein can comport itself in one way or another, and always does comport itself somehow, we call "existence"'(ibid., p. 32).

Then there follows a passage that tells us a great deal about how Heidegger understood 'existence':

> Dasein always understands itself in terms of its existence – in terms of a possibility of itself: to be itself or not itself. Dasein either has chosen these possibilities itself or got itself into them, or grown up in them already. Only the particular Dasein decides its existence, whether it does so by taking hold of or by neglecting. The question of existing never gets straightened out except through existing itself. (Ibid., p. 33)

This passage touches on some of the central themes of Heidegger's thinking. Dasein is not static – it has possibilities. It either finds itself thrown into them, or it has chosen them, but in either case it can realize them or put them aside. Possibilities suggest a temporal framework; they *are* not yet but may *be* in the future. Dasein alone has possibility and choice: this is the radical difference between human and other beings.

This is the reason why Heidegger uses the word 'existence' only for the Being of human beings. The word is derived from the Latin 'existere' which means 'standing out'. Human Being reaches out beyond itself, it is not fixed in itself like a rock is. It relates to its own existence, to the dimensions of time, to others, to the world.

Being and Dasein

The fact that the question of Being can only be pursued by an exploration of the Being of human beings is often seen as a detour, inevitable but still only a means to an end. Heidegger's main concern remained, after all, the meaning of Being as such, and not the Being of human beings, the existence of Dasein. But throughout his thinking Heidegger emphasized that Being and Dasein could not be separated, and this gives the exploration of existence a status far beyond digression. In Heidegger's later work, there is the implication that Being depends for its appearance on the 'there' (da) offered (or denied) to it by 'Da-sein'.

'Existentials'

Heidegger's exploration of existence, which is the main content of *Being and Time*, tries to find universal characteristics of existence, 'existentials' – and it is at this point that his relevance for psychotherapy emerges. (This was of course many years before he showed any interest in psychotherapy.) Here psychotherapists meet descriptions of conditions with which they are familiar from their own work: anxiety and guilt; relation to others; mortality. Whether Heidegger's descriptions of these conditions have anything to offer to the work of psychotherapists remains, of course, a question at this point.

So far we have followed a rather sketchy outline of Heidegger's way from his crucial question 'What is Being?' to the inseparable connection of this question with the Being of the only being for whom this Being is an *issue* and whom it concerns closely. But Heidegger's way led to psychotherapy also in a more literal sense – he was, so to speak, invited into it.

Heidegger and Binswanger

Before we turn to Heidegger's active participation in the creation of an existential framework for therapy, we need to say something about his relationship with Ludwig Binswanger, which preceded his contact with Medard Boss (who was to 'invite' him into psychotherapy) by many years. I owe my information to an important paper by Roger Frie, which was published in 1999 by the *Journal of the British Society of Phenomenology*. This paper uses the unpublished exchange of letters between Binswanger and Heidegger. These letters are preserved in the Binswanger Archive at the University of Tübingen to which Frie had access.

The start of this relationship is seen in a letter Heidegger wrote to Binswanger in 1928.

In this letter Heidegger asked Binswanger if he would like to make a donation for a bust of Husserl to celebrate the philosopher's seventieth birthday. Binswanger was glad to do so as he was a great admirer of Husserl whose concern with the 'phenomena' seemed to offer an answer to questions provoked in him by aspects of the psychoanalytic approach. Binswanger was a psychiatrist who had trained at the Burghölzli hospital under Bleuler and Jung, and he had become a lifelong friend of Freud.

Heidegger and Binswanger met for the first time in 1929 in Frankfurt, where Heidegger gave a lecture. What drew Binswanger to Heidegger was, above all, his view of human existence as 'Being-in-the-world', which came close to

Binswanger's desire to understand the total reality of the suffering of his patients. He wrote about this in a paper discussing the influence of Heidegger's analysis of Dasein on psychiatry:

> In thus indicating the basic structure of Dasein, Heidegger places in the psychiatrist's hands a methodological key by means of which he can, free of the prejudice of scientific theory, ascertain and describe phenomena he investigates in the full phenomenal content and context. (Frie, 1999, p. 246)

When Binswanger's main work *Grundformen und Erkenntnis menschlichen Daseins* (*Basic Forms and Understanding of Human Being-there*) appeared in 1944, he apprehensively wrote to Heidegger and prepared him for the critical comments contained in it. He stressed 'the difference between (Heidegger's) pure ontological intentions and (his own) anthropological endeavours' (ibid., p. 250). At the time Heidegger's response was, in fact, very appreciative: 'I thank you for the existence of your great work and that you have given it to me' (ibid.). We shall see that Heidegger's reaction to Binswanger's critique changed considerably by the time he mentioned it again in Zollikon.

Here is not the place to go more deeply into the fundamentally different approach of these two men, which in the earlier part of their contact did not seem to disturb their relationship. As was seen above Binswanger always made it quite clear that his concern was with what he called the 'anthropological' aspects of Being-in-the-world and not with the ontological dimension. Heidegger's main concern, on the other hand, was not anthropological (what he called 'ontic') but ontological – the question of Being as such. These two views can still be distinguished in existential therapy. We shall discuss in later chapters the distinction between the 'ontological', which describes aspects of Being itself, and the 'ontic', which describes particular and specific ways in which human beings live their Being day by day.

In 1947 Heidegger received a letter from Binswanger. This

letter was a reply to Heidegger's suggestion that he should 'write a hermeneutics of exploration' (ibid., p. 251) based on his clinical experience. Binswanger replied enthusiastically: 'I am now looking especially forward to entering into a dialogue with you, and already have the impression it will be a beginning without end' (ibid.).

Boss approaches Heidegger

In the same year, a Swiss psychoanalyst, Medard Boss, also wrote to Martin Heidegger. For some time Boss had been looking for a different philosophical foundation for his work. He had tried to read *Being and Time*, but as Condrau reports (Condrau, 1998, p. 126), he had found the book difficult to comprehend and turned to the writer for help. The problem that particularly occupied Boss was that of 'Time'.

Boss tells us how surprised he was 'to receive an answer by return of post' (Heidegger, 1987, p. xi; all quotations from this publication are translated by the author). Heidegger was prepared to give him whatever help was possible. This was the first of a series of 256 letters, which marked the beginning of their friendship and only ended with Heidegger's death. Why this new friendship extinguished Heidegger's contact with Binswanger so completely, we do not know, but we are free to wonder about it. The publication of the correspondence between Heidegger and Binswanger would, no doubt, answer some questions.

What was the reason for Heidegger's eagerness? Boss reports:

> The most important motive behind his quick reply revealed itself much later. Martin Heidegger confessed to me that from the very beginning he expected much from the connection with a medical practitioner who in many ways seemed to understand his own thinking. He saw a possibility that his philosophical insights might not remain stuck in the attics of philosophers, but might benefit a much greater number of people, particularly those in need of help. (Ibid., p. x)

The Zollikon Seminars

Heidegger went to visit Boss frequently in his house in Zollikon, and eventually seminars were worked into these visits. They gave 'friends, colleagues and students' of Boss 'a sound philosophical foundation for [their] medical activities' as Boss put it (ibid., p. xi). These seminars lasted from 1959 to 1969, though they were only protocolled from 1964 by Boss himself. These protocols were sent to Heidegger, who corrected them and returned them.

The *Zollikoner Seminare* have not yet been translated, and very little has been written about them. Their German publication in 1987 has an introduction by Boss, and he adds to the seminar protocols a number of fragments of conversations between himself and Heidegger as well as a selection of their letters. There is a certain carelessness about this book that does an injustice to its importance. For instance, it lacks a proper index and provides very few notes. Some thorough research into the occasion and themes of the *Zollikoner Seminare* would be most desirable.

At this point I shall only give a short overview of Heidegger's teaching and discussions at the time. This will show that Heidegger (who had meanwhile acquainted himself with the basic aspects of Freudian theory) was genuinely concerned with seeing the problems of psychotherapy in the light of his own philosophical thought.

The *Zollikon Seminars* offer psychotherapists essentially an introduction to Heidegger's thinking. It is interesting that he bases a great deal of his exposition on *Being and Time*, his earliest major work which, as we have seen, concerns itself with the specific aspects of human existence or Dasein. This contradicts the frequently held assumption of a radical break between Heidegger's early and later writing. Going back to a work written more than thirty years before he started teaching students and therapists in Zollikon shows that Heidegger still acknowledged his original insights as the roots from which his later thinking had grown.

Heidegger's teaching and the discussions arising from it cover the following main themes:

1. The difference between phenomena and explanation.
2. The difference between Being (Sein) and beings (das Seiende).
3. Aspects of Time (a topic that is discussed at great length).
4. Aspects of Space.
5. The body/mind question (a problem Heidegger hardly touched on in *Being and Time*).
6. Descartes and natural science.
7. The subject/object question.
8. What is 'Daseinsanalyse'?

Throughout the philosophical presentation, which has, on the whole, much greater simplicity than in *Being and Time*, there are references to the kinds of situations psychotherapists and psychiatrists are likely to meet. These themes will be discussed at various points.

What is 'Daseinsanalyse'?

It was Binswanger, having been in contact with Heidegger since 1927 (the year *Being and Time* was published), who first used the term 'Daseinsanalyse' (analysis of Being-there). He described it as the introduction of the phenomenological approach into the practice of psychiatry. In the words of Gion Condrau (who wrote an interesting overview of the history of 'Daseinsanalyse'):

> Binswanger saw the Daseinsanalytic task of psychiatry as the understanding of the structure of Dasein of a specific individual person, without a distinction between 'healthy' and 'sick', 'normal' and 'abnormal'. He criticized very sharply the assumption that there was no meaning to be found in the minds of patients who were mentally ill. (Condrau, 1998, pp. 11–12 – my translation)

Binswanger may have been influenced by Heidegger's use of the word 'Daseinsanalytik'. But as we have seen, he was well aware that Heidegger's 'Daseinsanalytik' was an ontological exploration of Being itself, while Binswanger's 'Daseinsanalyse' dealt with the understanding of 'specific individual persons'. Binswanger did not see his 'Daseinsanalyse' as a new therapy, rather, he was concerned with a fuller description of his patient's existence, but he did not discuss the consequences this approach might have for the practice of 'Daseinsanalyse'.

'After the second world war, another school of "Daseinsanalyse" formed itself in Zurich which deviated from Binswanger and whose primary concern was the application of Heidegger's teaching to the theory of neuroses and psychotherapy' (ibid., p. 12). This was indeed a new form of therapy, still based to some extent on Freud, for instance, his use of the couch, accepting his practice though rejecting his 'meta-psychology'. Condrau touches on the question of such a separation of practice from theory:

> Originally it seemed as if [Daseinsanalyse] distinguished itself only or predominantly in its theoretical superstructure from psychoanalysis, in its philosophical foundation and anthropological interpretations of existence. But increasingly it became clear that theory and practice could never be completely separated from each other. (Ibid., p. 15)

It is one of the aims of this book to show that such separation is, in fact, always impossible.

Heidegger's view of 'Daseinsanalyse'

How did Heidegger see 'Daseinsanalyse' at a time when he was an important participant in its establishment as an existential therapy? In Zollikon he was emphatic in his distinction between 'Daseinsanalytik' and 'Daseinsanalyse'. 'Daseinsanalyse is ontic, Daseinsanalytik ontological' (Heidegger, 1987, p. 161).

He adds: 'Daseinsanalytik is . . . an ontological interpretation of being human, and serves to prepare the question of Being' (ibid., p. 162). And he states: 'From this "Daseinsanalyse" needs to be fundamentally distinguished when it is the demonstration and description of phenomena which are shown factually by a definite existing Dasein' (ibid., p. 163).

Does this now mean that an existential therapy that is developed within the framework of Heidegger's ideas can only be ontic? This is a question that we shall discuss at a later point. But we need to remember that Heidegger emphasizes that human beings have in common the concern for their own Being, and this concern is always included in what they are and do even if they are not aware of it. There is always a link between the ontic and the ontological.

Heidegger's involvement with the Nazis

There is one other aspect of Heidegger's 'way' to psychotherapy I wish to consider. We have heard of Boss's surprise when Heidegger answered his letter by return of post. Boss also tells us that 'the most important motive behind (Heidegger's) quick reply revealed itself much later'. According to Boss, Heidegger expressed the hope that his views 'might benefit a much greater number of people, particularly those in need of help'. These are Boss's words. But if, in fact, Heidegger said anything like that, it seems indeed surprising as the comment from a man who had shown so little sensitivity and concern for the suffering and the fate of others.

At the time Boss contacted Heidegger not a great deal of Heidegger's involvement with Hitler and National Socialism was widely known. It was the books of Hugo Ott (1994), Victor Farias (1989) and Richard Wolin (1993) which made the world familiar with the dark and chilling aspects of Heidegger's participation in the establishment of Nazi rule, particularly at the Universities. However we try to understand this and whatever theories have been put forward to explain it, Heidegger's silence about the suffering and the deaths of Hitler's victims has been almost universally condemned. George Steiner, a great admirer of Heidegger's thinking, has put it very simply: 'But nauseating as they are, Heidegger's gestures and pronouncements during 1933/4 are tractable. It is his complete silence on Hitlerism and the holocaust after 1945 which is very nearly intolerable' (Steiner, 1992, p. 123).

For people who only know *Being and Time*, there seems an unbridgeable gap between Heidegger's thinking in 1927 and his strident pronouncement to students and colleagues six years later which seemed to hail the arrival of Hitler as an answer to Heidegger's philosophical concerns. But some writers have shown that during these six years a distortion and vulgarization of Heidegger's thinking had taken place which made the transformation from existential thinker to Nazi spokesman, if not less extraordinary, at least less puzzling.

This is not the place to go into the details of his philosophical self-betrayal (as I see it) but a few observations are necessary for our assessment of his eventual turning to psychotherapy. Anybody who wishes to study the many-layered sleight of hand that led from the existential phenomenology of *Being and Time* to the infamous rectoral address at Freiburg in 1933 can do so in Caputo's *Demythologizing Heidegger* (1993), or more briefly in Polt's introduction to Heidegger (Polt, 1999, pp. 133ff.). After *Being and Time* Heidegger's *question* of Being turned into a *myth* of Being which Heidegger calls 'history'. Originally Heidegger emphasized that Being as such was indescribable, it was not a quality, it simply indicated the difference between something being and or not being: the difference, say, between 'there is a rock' and 'there is no rock'. Perhaps it is important to know that 'there is' in German is 'es gibt'. 'Gibt' has the same root as 'gift'. The meaning of Being is here the 'givenness' of beings, no more, no less. There is also the implication of the question whether what is 'given', a 'gift', requires a response.

By 1933 the meaning of Being had changed. In Polt's book we find a summary of this change (1999, p. 132). Heidegger tells us that in Ancient Greece (before Plato and Aristotle) there was a general openness to Being but gradually neglect and forgetting set in which led to an increasing concealment of Being.

As in many myths, salvation is possible, and it is Dasein with its potential openness to all that *is* which can offer its 'there' for the return of Being. It is at this point that Heidegger makes his crudest changes to his original existential analysis of Dasein. Dasein is no longer your or my Dasein, but the Dasein of a nation – the German nation that is assumed to have a mythical link – Heidegger calls it 'historical' – with the Greeks.

This is, of course, a very sketchy summary of a complex web of thought. But no matter how well we know its meshes, it remains, in my view, a strip-cartoon version of *Being and Time*. However, it also offers a suitable metaphysical background for Heidegger's welcoming of Hitler and the Nazis, with the absurd assumption that it is they who will – with a collective 'authenticity' (see Chapter 11) – be the 'there' for a return of Being. By doing this the German people will save the Western world from certain perdition. Hitler as a St George fighting the dragon of the loss of Being – gruesome though this scenario is – has also elements of the grotesque and the ridiculous.

After about a year Heidegger came to realize that the Nazis did not see their aim in this way. On the other hand they found this philosopher, whose fame seemed originally to recommend his involvement, an unintelligible, dominating and potentially dangerous ally. Separation became inevitable. Though Heidegger seems to have continued to be a party member until 1945, the party political element disappeared from the myth of Being; what remains is the inseparable interdependence of Being and Dasein with which he started out.

The link between *Being and Time* and the *Zollikon Seminars*

At this point, I hope the aim of my fragmentary and oversimplified digression may become clear. I think in the lectures to students and psychiatrists in Zollikon the myth of Being has faded remarkably, and there is a return to existential phenomenology, the 'hermeneutics of facticity' of his early work. A great deal of what he says is a repetition of and a commentary on the basic ideas of *Being and Time*, often more lucidly expressed.

The way to psychotherapy started, as we have seen, by Heidegger's realization that the question 'What is Being?' can only be answered by exploring the human situation: for only human beings are concerned with their Being, can reflect on it, have something to say about it.

Progress on this way seemed to become fatally disrupted when Heidegger ceased to keep the question of Being open and instead 'essentialized' it, as Caputo (1993, pp. 118ff.) puts it, by separating it from concrete existence and giving it an origin and a history of gradual decline due to human neglect. Thus in Heidegger's eyes his affiliation with the Nazi movement becomes a call for the restoration of Being. Being becomes a kind of fallen Godhead that depends on human intervention for its return.

Surprisingly and mysteriously, Heidegger, in the end, returned to his own beginnings, to the phenomena, to his original aim 'to let that which shows itself be seen from itself in the very way in which it shows itself from itself' (Heidegger, 1962, p. 58). This return can be seen in his lectures in Zollikon.

An unanswerable question

For me there arises an unanswerable question: How far did Heidegger's return to the greater openness of his earlier thinking reflect a realization of his philosophical self-betrayal? How far does his unexpected concern for people in need of help and for the task of psychotherapists reveal something of the shame and guilt regarding his involvement with National Socialism that he never expressed? In the face of his silence such an assumption must remain hypothetical.

Among the few indications we have of how Heidegger felt about his alliance with the Nazis the following comments by Parvis Emad in his introduction to H. W. Petzet's memoir of Heidegger seem important:

> Heidegger was profoundly ashamed of having been associated with the Nazis. In two letters to Karl Jaspers, dated 7 March 1950 and 8 April 1950, Heidegger speaks of his shame. In the letter of April 8 he sums up what he has communicated to Jaspers 'What I report here can excuse nothing. Rather, it can explain how, when over the course of years what is virulently evil (das Bösartige) became manifest, my shame grew – the shame of directly or indirectly having been involved in it'. (Petzet, 1993, p. xxxi)

Though this letter to Jaspers is significant, it does not amount to a public admission of guilt. One thing seems certain: if Heidegger had not returned, in the end, to his original thinking about the priority of phenomena, existential therapy would be much the poorer. And this book would certainly not have been written.

3 | Existence as Being-in-the-world

IN SEPTEMBER 1959 Martin Heidegger started his seminars for Medard Boss's colleagues and psychiatric students with a drawing that showed five half circles, each entered by an arrow: (< . Heidegger chalked this drawing onto the blackboard of the big auditorium of the Burghölzli Hospital where the first seminar took place. He wrote a short commentary about it that is worth looking at:

> This drawing is meant to show that human existence is essentially never just an object that is somewhere present, least of all an object closed in itself. Rather this existence consists of 'mere' potentialities – neither visible nor tangible – to perceive and be aware of all that encounters and addresses us. (Heidegger, 1987, p. 3)

The emphasis is on fluidity, potentiality and openness of existence, its basic incompleteness, and Heidegger goes on to compare this view with the more object-like, mechanistic 're-presentations' which dominate most psychological systems:

> All the usual capsule-like representations (common at present in psychology and psychopathology) of a psyche, a subject, a person, an Ego, a consciousness have – in an existential approach – to be relinquished and give way to a fundamentally different understanding. (Ibid.)

Heidegger next outlines how he perceives the essence of human existence and reaches, with the well-known term 'Being-in-the-world', a formulation which deviates more radically from the generally accepted view of Western thinking than may at first appear:

> The new 'ground' of human existence should be called 'Da-sein' (Being there) or 'Being-in-the-world'. The 'there' of this Being-there does, however, not mean – as it does colloquially – a position in space near to the viewer. Rather existence as 'Da-sein' means the opening up of a sphere where the sense of what is given can be perceived. Human 'Da-sein' – as a sphere of potentiality of perception and awareness – is never an object that is just present. It is, on the contrary, under no circumstances something that can be objectified. (Ibid., pp. 3–4)

This is an important text, and we shall return to it as many aspects of an existential therapy find roots in the 'ground' laid bare here. The links with the basic ideas of *Being and Time* are clear, though these ideas seem to me more lucidly expressed. Whatever the degree of 'turning' that is commonly seen as splitting Heidegger into an 'earlier' and 'later' thinker, we are witnessing in his *Zollikon Seminars* (all subsequent meetings took place in Boss's house in Zollikon) a 'return' to his beginnings, though modified and transformed

Most importantly, that is true for his concern with a phenomenological approach that he is often thought to have abandoned in his later writings. For seeing 'Being-there' 'as a sphere where the sense of what is given can be perceived' is the return to a phenomenology of existence which Heidegger – as a transformation of Husserl's phenomenology – had introduced into *Being and Time*.

Husserl and Heidegger

A brief consideration of the difference between Husserl and Heidegger's use of phenomenology may throw some light on the radical nature of Heidegger's view of existence as 'Being-in-the-world'. Husserl attempted to reach the essence of experience by finding a method 'to strip away the variants of experience and so to arrive at a clearer understanding of its invariants'. This method had the task to suspend 'as far as possible, the plethora of interpretational layers added to the unknown stimuli to our experience in order to arrive at a more adequate, if still approximate and incomplete, knowledge of "the things themselves"' (Spinelli, 1989, p. 16).

This meant the 'bracketing' of all assumptions (personal, cultural, philosophical and scientific), including the 'empirical' (that is experiencing) ego itself, in short: all that Heidegger would call 'world'. And this is the point where Heidegger was bound to disagree.

For Heidegger 'world' was the totality of everything human beings were involved in, 'all that encounters and addresses' them, as he put it in his comment on his drawing.

> Heidegger wanted to employ phenomenology as the proper mode of access to the phenomena of concrete human life, factical life, as he had initially called it in his early lecture courses, a way of thinking about human nature that remained faithful to the *historical, lived,* practical nature of human experience.
> (Moran, 2000, pp. 227–8; emphasis in the original)

For Heidegger human beings found themselves always 'thrown' into a world from which they were not separable. The world could not be bracketed. Existence is always a Being-in-the-world. The world is our context.

The Cartesian view

The existential-phenomenological understanding of human life as Being-in-the-world, with its emphasis on interconnectedness and interdependence, challenges a view dominant in a great deal of Western thinking. This sees the world as made up of beings and things that are essentially separate and independent entities, which are capable of joining variously in different forms of interaction.

This view is commonly traced back to the philosophy of René Descartes, and some aspects of it have become known as the 'mind/body problem' and the 'subject/object split'. I do not believe that one philosopher's view is likely to have had so wide-ranging an influence unless it reflects what many people already feel, however inarticulately. Also the tendency to split off different aspects of being from each other goes right back to the Greek roots of Western thinking and can be found in Plato and Aristotle.

Human beings tend to take apart what they wish to understand, examine the parts and feel disappointed when an understanding of the parts does not help to comprehend their context. In contrast to this tendency we shall see that particularly in psychotherapy, the context claims a priority over its parts. We neglect it at our peril.

Descartes's influence may be due to the uncompromising directness with which he expressed his belief in the radical separation of the individual being from whatever else there is in the world. In his search for certainty he came to doubt everything except the capacity for doubt, that is for thought. By doing so he tore open a gap between the 'thinking non-extended thing' – what we call 'mind' – and whatever it was encountering. This gap he illustrated poignantly by his emphatic distinction between mind and body:

> On the one hand, I have a clear and distinct idea of myself in so far as I am simply a thinking, non-extended thing, and on the other

> hand, I have a clear and distinct idea of body in so far as this is simply an extended, non-thinking thing. (Cottingham, 1993, p. 124)

Non-extension and extension are not only the essential characteristics of mind and body, but those of the mind and the world in general – and all 'extended non-thinking things', according to Descartes, obey the laws of mechanics. Descartes expresses this view with great lucidity:

> I do not recognize any difference between artifacts and natural bodies, except that the operations of artifacts are for the most part brought about by mechanisms that are large enough to be easily perceived by the senses ... The effects produced in nature, by contrast, always depend on structures, which are so minute that they completely elude our senses. (Ibid., p. 111)

> Growth, digestion, respiration, the reception of sensory data, the internal movements of the appetites and the external movement of the limbs, [can all be explained as] following from the mere arrangements of the machine's organs as naturally as the movement of a clock or other automaton follows the arrangement of its counterweight and wheels. (Ibid., p. 112)

Let us sum up the picture of human existence as it emerges from Descartes's considerations. Human beings have minds and bodies, but these are quite divorced from each other. Only a human being has a mind – 'a thinking thing . . . is for Descartes a self-conscious, language-using being, capable in principle of reflecting on its own nature and existence', as Cottingham puts it (ibid., p. 5). Animals therefore have no minds.

Most importantly, however, though human beings have minds, each mind can grasp with any certainty only one thing: itself. For there is, of course, also a gap between one mind and other minds.

A disembodied mind separated from a world machine and unable to reach anything with certainty except itself seems a long way from human existence seen as 'Being-in-the-world'. Let us recall that Heidegger in his first communication to his students in Switzerland describes human existence as always part and in the midst of the world, a potentiality 'to perceive and be aware of all that encounters and addresses it'. Instead of separation we have here perception and an opening up in a context of mutuality.

The subject/object split

Heidegger makes it quite clear that he sees his existential phenomenology as a response to Descartes's separation of mind from world. In his Swiss lectures he presents this separation as the split between subject and object:

> Greek and medieval thinking does not yet know the concept of object and objectivity . . . Objectivity is a modification of the presence of things. The presence of things is here understood as the presentation to a subject. Things are no longer accepted as they give themselves but are opposed to me as a thinking subject, 'objected' into me. This kind of experience of being is with us only since Descartes, that is, since human beings have been turned into subjects. (Heidegger, 1987, p. 129)

The important distinction in this passage is that between 'presence' (Anwesenheit) and 'presentation' (Vorgestelltheit). Phenomena are 'things as they present themselves'. Their presentation to a subject objectifies them. Heidegger goes on to say:

> The fundamental difference is that earlier experience saw what *is* only as present in itself. But for modern experience something *is* only in relation to a presentation of it. Modern science is the change of experience from something present [anwesend] into something objective [gegenständlich]. (Ibid.)

Measurability

To Heidegger making the world 'objective' means making it measurable, a necessary step on our way to mastering it:

> Measurability means, in fact, being open to calculations. It is an approach to nature which enables us to know what natural processes we can and must anticipate ... And anticipation is desirable if the aim is the domination of natural processes. But domination includes nature's availability to us, a kind of owning it. In the final section of his fundamental *Discours de la Methode* Descartes sees the aim of science as 'nous rendre comme maitres et possesseurs de la nature'. (Ibid., pp. 135–6)

Being 'the masters and owners of nature' is, however, the opposite to letting 'that which shows itself be seen from itself in the very way in which it shows itself from itself' (Heidegger, 1962, p. 58), as Heidegger defines the phenomenon in *Being and Time*. The 'anticipation' and 'domination' of nature is different from the readiness 'to perceive and be aware of all that encounters and addresses us' (Heidegger, 1987, p. 3). By objectifying the phenomena, we are making them 'useful' but are destroying what they are as such. Heidegger believed that by 'mastering' the phenomena rather than meeting them we are dangerously unbalancing the context of Dasein and Being.

This is controversial territory in which science and technology will argue their case. Similar questions arise, however, from our concern with threats to our environment, or our fear of genetic manipulation. In this book we need to consider the relevance of Heidegger's warning to the process of therapeutic interaction.

Heidegger's view of science

Heidegger is often accused of being opposed to the sciences. There can be no doubt that he was afraid of technology with its roots in scientific 'measurability' which leads to the objectifying and 'mastering' of phenomena. Heidegger questions the suitability of science to approach those aspects of being human that cannot be objectified, anticipated, calculated, 'mastered'. In his Swiss lectures he repeatedly returned to this theme:

> It is the method which decides what is an object for science and how alone it can be made accessible . . . It is not primarily nature as it addresses human beings out of itself that is decisive, but the image of nature held by human beings when it is rooted in their intention to rule it. (Ibid., p. 32)

> Natural science can define human beings only as part of the natural world. The question arises: can human existence be met in this way? . . . The question remains: What is more important – the scientific method of comprehending and calculating regularities and rules, or the necessity to define the existence of human beings by the way in which they are experiencing it? (Ibid.)

For Heidegger, human beings could not be defined biologically. (In his later writings and the Swiss lectures, Heidegger uses the word 'Mensch' which covers both genders and which I translate as 'human beings'.) The essence of being human was to Heidegger 'existence' – and that meant an openness to the world, a readiness to be addressed and to address the phenomena as they show themselves. This is the meaning of the expression 'existential phenomenology', and its distinction from other phenomenological approaches.

Therapeutic relevance

If, with Heidegger, we choose to see the Cartesian separation of mind and world as a split between subject and object, our question is then: what is the relevance of Heidegger's warning against this split for the process of psychotherapy?

1. The relationship between therapist and client cannot be that of 'observer' and 'observed' but has the characteristics of 'Being-in-the-world' and the mutuality of 'Being-with' (to which we shall return in the following chapter). If there is no gap to bridge between a 'subject' and an 'object', the interaction between therapist and client – as any interaction between human beings – is direct and need not be explained by ingenious though strained mechanistic constructions like transference and introjection. The phenomena that give rise to such explanations need to be understood in the total context of the therapeutic situation.
2. Therapy cannot have a 'secure frame' with rigid rules in order to exclude contaminations with 'variables' (as would be necessary in a laboratory experiment) but needs the flexibility to take the uniqueness of each therapeutic context into account.
3. The space for therapy is not 'inside' a subject with the exclusion of the world, what Heidegger calls 'the capsule-like representation of a psyche', but the world itself which the client inhabits and in turn helps to create. This world includes, of course, the therapist.
4. Most importantly, therapists cannot, like scientists, impose their explanatory expectations on the phenomena, with diagnostic labels and reductive interpretations, but keep open to what the phenomena themselves are telling them.

4 | Existence as 'Being-with'

What is Being-with?

'Being-with' is an aspect of 'Being-in-the-world': 'the world is always the one I share with others. The world of Dasein is a with-world' (Heidegger, 1962, p. 155). Heidegger has often been accused of not being concerned for people's actual relationships, and it is true that – with a few important exceptions to which we shall return – he chose to say little about them. This may lead us to undervalue the importance of his concept of 'Being-with' as an aspect of existence as such. A literal translation of 'Mitsein' as 'With-being' would be perhaps bring this out more clearly.

We need here, as always, to distinguish the ontological aspect from its ontic manifestations. 'Being-with is an existential characteristic of Dasein even when factically no Other is present-at-hand or perceived' (ibid., p. 156). What Heidegger calls here an 'existential characteristic' he generally refers to as an 'existentiale' (often translated as 'existential'). Being-with is an aspect of Dasein whether, in fact (that is 'ontically'), anybody else happens to be there or not. We are always 'with' others, whether we take notice of this or not. The individual can never be understood in isolation. Heidegger emphasizes this distinction between the ontological and the ontic even more clearly in a later passage. 'Even if the particular factical Dasein does *not* turn to Others, and supposes it has no need of them or manages to get along without them, it *is* in the way of Being-with' (ibid., p. 160).

It is important to remain aware of this distinction, as colloquially 'being with someone' implies certain qualities of concern, understanding and empathy, which are only a particular ontic way of living our 'Being-with'. Putting it differently: finding ourselves existentially in a position of 'With-being', we face the question of how to respond to it.

Heidegger's difficulty with Binswanger

Heidegger illustrates the importance of this distinction when he talks in his Swiss seminars – which often clarify the dense definitions in *Being and Time* – about his disagreement with the psychiatrist Ludwig Binswanger.

Heidegger pointed out that Binswanger had misunderstood his use of the word 'Sorge', an 'existential' closely connected to 'Being-with', though somewhat misleadingly translated as 'care', which again carries colloquially rooted meanings that Heidegger did not intend. 'Concern' or 'involvement' might be more helpful translations. Let us hear what Heidegger had to say:

> Ludwig Binswanger had to admit a few years ago that he had misunderstood [my] Daseinsanalytik, though he called his mistake productive. Thus you will find in Binswanger's great book on the basic forms of Dasein a 'supplement' to Heidegger's 'bleak care' in the shape of a treatise on love which, according to Binswanger, Heidegger had forgotten. (Heidegger, 1987, p. 151)

Heidegger goes on to say:

> Binswanger's misunderstanding does not consist so much in his wish to supplement care with love, but in the fact that he does not see that the meaning of 'care' is existential, ontological, and that 'Daseinsanalyse' explores its ontological (existential) foundation

> and does not wish to give a description of ontic phenomena. (Ibid., p. 151)

Heidegger sees 'love' as one possible ontic manifestation of the fundamental involvement with others, which is the existential meaning of Being-with. When Heidegger speaks ontologically, he discusses universal aspects of human existence, say 'care', and not their ontic manifestations, say 'love'. This does not mean he has 'forgotten' love.

Human relationships

In another Swiss seminar, held in the same year as the one that brought his confrontation with Binswanger, Heidegger unfolded an ontological analysis of 'Beziehungen' between human beings (this is usually translated as 'relationships'):

> First of all, we need to ask: How are other human beings 'there'? Do you relate to other human beings as you relate to the glass on the table in front of you? Such talk of relating, of our relationships with other human beings, or between human beings, is misleading because it seduces us into imagining two separate subjects who are assumed to make connections between representations of themselves in their respective consciousness. Seen in this way, the concept of 'relation' tends to obscure an engagement with how we truly are with others.
>
> However, how are we with each other? Is it the case that in this room there is somebody here, and another over there, and there is also one of us present – and then we just add each other up? This notion is clearly false, but a widely known psychological theory of empathy is based on it. This imagines, in a purely Cartesian manner, an independent 'I' that then feels its way into someone else and discovers that this person is a human being as well, an 'alter ego'. This is, however, only a construction …
>
> When we talk readily about I- and Thou-, and We-relations, we

> talk about something very incomplete. This way of talking has its origin still in an 'I' that is primarily isolated. (Ibid., pp. 144–5)

I quote Heidegger's Swiss lecture on 'Being-with' rather fully, as I have not come across another passage in his writings in which he talks about its ontological status as lucidly. As the Swiss seminars are still inaccessible to readers who do not know German, readers are bound to find themselves puzzled by some of Heidegger's short references to this theme at various places. Here he sums up his view on 'Being-with' with unmistakable clarity:

> We need to ask: Where, and what am I with, when I am with you? It is a 'Being-with', and that means: I exist with you in the way of 'Being-in-the-world', and particularly a being-with-each-other in our relation to whatever encounters us.
>
> As each of us is a Dasein as Being-in-the-world, being-with-each-other cannot mean anything but a being-with-each-other-in-the-world. Thus I am, first of all, not related to your presence as an individual but dwell with you in the same Being-here. Being-with-each-other is not the relation of one subject to another. (Ibid., p. 145)

Heidegger is not 'first of all' concerned with the specific ('ontic') relations between individuals but with the fact that as existing human beings we share the same world, and as 'Dasein' we are similarly open to whatever encounters us. This is an existential relatedness which precedes any particuar relationship.

This does not mean that Heidegger does not distinguish between different ways of 'Being-with', Heidegger concludes the seminar from which I have taken my long quotation with a comparison:

> Imagine as an example the situation that we are sitting in a restaurant, each of us alone at a different table. Are we then not with-each-other? Yes, we are, but in a very different way than here

> where we talk to each other. Sitting on one's own in the restaurant is a privation of a being-with-each-other. Here the existing beings have nothing to do with each other, and this is their way of being-with-each-other in the same room. (Ibid., pp. 145–6)

Ontologically, we cannot but 'be with' others, but how we do this is another matter. Does Heidegger evaluate these different responses? This is a difficult question that arises frequently in his writings. Here, the use of the word 'privation' – and this is his own word, and is the same in German and English – seems to indicate that he does. Let us not forget that his philosophical quest started with the pronouncement that 'Being' has been forgotten, and he clearly saw this as a lack.

Two forms of solicitude

Perhaps we need to look at the frequently quoted passage about two forms of 'solicitude' in *Being and Time* in a similar way. 'Solicitude' (Fürsorge) is related to 'Care' (Sorge), and describes, as Heidegger says, 'the concern of one Dasein for another Dasein' (Heidegger, 1962, p.158). Heidegger also distinguishes 'deficient modes of solicitude': thus, being 'against, or without one another, passing one another by, "not mattering" to one another – these are possible ways of solicitude' (ibid., p. 158). We are reminded of Heidegger's characterization of Being-with as an aspect of existence 'even if no other is present-at-hand or perceived' (ibid., p. 156). The word 'deficient' seems to me a clear evaluation of such a response, and how it is not 'there' for what encounters it.

Against such a 'deficient' response Heidegger puts explicitly 'two positive modes' of solicitude:

> It can, as it were, take away 'care' from the Other and put itself in his position in concern: it can *leap in* for him. This kind of solicitude takes over for the Other that with which he is to concern himself. The Other is thus thrown out of his own position; he

> steps back so that afterwards, when the matter has been attended to, he can either take it over as something finished and at his disposal, or disburden himself of it completely. (Ibid., p. 158)

From this Heidegger distinguishes:

> A kind of solicitude which does not so much leap in for the Other as *leap ahead* of him in his existentiell potentiality for Being, not in order to take away his 'care' but rather to give it back to him authentically for the first time. (Ibid., p. 159)

These two modes of solicitude are illustrated by two kinds of therapies – those that support clients by advice or medication, and those that help them understand their situation and their part in it.

Has one of these modes greater validity than the other? Heidegger calls them both 'positive'. On the other hand, we are led by the use of the word 'authentic' (eigentlich) to believe that Heidegger gives greater value to the 'leaping ahead' form of solicitude. We shall return to a consideration of what Heidegger means by 'eigentlich' (authentic). (See Chapter 11.)

But it seems unquestionable that Heidegger especially values this kind of solicitude as it concerns the Other's 'existentiell potentiality-for-Being'. Any realization of the potentiality-for-Being, the opening up towards all that is and addresses us, is, in Heidegger's view, at the core of human existence, and a Being-with that helps to make this possible for the Other is an affirmation of Being-in-the-world.

The question of ethics

Heidegger has often been accused of neglecting to spell out the ethical implications of his thinking, and this accusation gains support from his unjustifiable and intolerable involvement with the Nazi movement. There is, in fact, at times, a strange ambivalence in his writings when he seems to present us only with potentialities of existence without recommending which to realize, while at the same time making it clear enough what his values are.

One thing is certain: all his philosophical thought is centred in his regret of human 'forgetfulness of Being' (Seinsvergessenheit), and he advocates explicitly or implicitly whatever we can do to end it.

In his book *Heidegger and the Ground of Ethics* (1998) Olafson attempts to base an ethics on Heidegger's thoughts on 'Being-with'. He takes as his point of departure a sentence Medard Boss recollected from one of his conversations with Heidegger at the time of the Zollikon seminars. 'To be subject to the claim that presence makes is the greatest claim that a human being makes; it is what "ethics" is' (Olafson, 1998, p. 1). (The grammar of the German sentence is ambiguous. I am inclined to think that it is the 'presence' that makes a claim on human beings!)

The problem with this sentence for Olafson is that though 'it explicitly connects presence (Anwesenheit) with ethics . . . it does not acknowledge the even more important connection of ethics with reciprocal presence and thus with "Mitsein" (Being-with)'. For Olafson, the ethical questions arise when the presences are Daseins – 'entities that can recognize one another as bearers of truth and relate to one another in a manner that in one way or another presupposes this fact' (ibid., p. 100). The truth is here the openness that these Daseins share with each other.

But is Heidegger, in fact, quite as unaware of 'reciprocal presence'? We have seen that he is not. Heidegger calls sitting alone in a restaurant with others, who also sit on their own, a 'privation' of Being-with when compared with a discussion in a seminar. Here he seems to be aware of just what Olafson calls a 'reciprocal presence', and it appears that an evaluation is made, even if we might not call it 'ethical'. We also saw Heidegger comparing 'positive' with 'deficient' modes of solicitude, and solicitude is clearly a form of 'reciprocal presence'. Indeed such examples support Olafson's view, which I share, that there is a 'ground for ethics' to be found in Heidegger's ontological approach to 'Being-with'.

Therapeutic relevance

1. The individual living in a 'with-world' can never be understood in isolation – s/he has to be seen in the context of her/his 'with-being'. As the context is in constant flux, the image of a fixed 'internal' psychic structure is a construction. The qualities (including 'privations' and 'deficiencies') of the 'reciprocal presence' of individuals needs exploration.
2. When Heidegger, in his Swiss seminars, describes the usual talk of 'relations with other human beings' as 'misleading' because it assumes 'connections between representations' we are reminded of his indictment of 'all the usual objectifying capsule-like representations (common at present in psychology and psychopathology) of a psyche . . . ' (Heidegger, 1987, p. 3).

   Heidegger asks 'where, and what am I with, when I am with you? It is a "being with", and that means: I exist with you in the way of "Being-in-the-world", particularly a being-with-each-other in our relation to whatever encounters us' (ibid., p. 145). For the therapeutic situation, this means a more direct communication between therapist and client who share a world and are 'with each other' in what they meet. There is no need for assuming the mediating scaffolding of 'representations' like 'projections' and 'transference'.
3. Another way of expressing the 'with'-character of human existence is by saying that the individual is a priori the member of a group – a group of two, at first, which however implies from the very beginning an ever-growing number of human beings. Though all of us experience this, in our culture we prefer to think of ourselves as self-sufficient entities that may or may not join others. Most therapeutic groups see themselves in this way, and strangely enough an

existential approach to group work has been neglected (cf. Cohn, 1997a, chapter 5).

4. When clients bring their difficulties with relationships to therapists they rarely see them as a distortion or neglect of a potentiality which all human beings possess – the capacity to relate to others. An existential approach can open up the shift from a paralysing conviction of incapacity (I cannot relate/you cannot relate) to an attempt to explore their ways of realizing possibilities which are aspects of existence itself.
5. Finally, the 'with-world' is a world of context, connections, mutuality and change in which you cannot 'pin-point' anything or look for single causes, specific origins and unique events. 'With-being' is a web with many strands, each of which is potentially relevant.

5 | Language as Being-with

The meaning of language

Anna O, the first patient who experienced the psychoanalytic approach – as a patient not of Freud but of his friend Breuer – called it the 'talking cure'. This was a significant description that became widely accepted: it emphasized the fact that healing was achieved without medication. Talking has always been a central characteristic of psychotherapy though its meaning and purpose have varied.

Heidegger was concerned with the meaning of language throughout his life – he introduces it into the context of *Being and Time*, and returns to it in the *Zollikon Seminars*. He presents it as an aspect of Being-with which, as we have seen, he regards as an 'existential'. This notion of language goes beyond the spoken word and opens up a new dimension to psychotherapists.

Stress as an aspect of talk

Talking about language to his psychiatric audience, he took 'stress' as his point of departure:

> Stress is fundamentally the demand that is made when someone is addressed. This is only possible on the basis of language. Language is here not understood as the ability to inform but as the original

> way of opening up what *is*, sustained by human beings in various forms. To the extent to which a human being is Being-with, that is, essentially related to other human beings, language as such is talk [Gespräch]. (Heidegger, 1987, p. 183)

Later Heidegger continues (cf. Chapter 6, pp. 54f.):

> . . . stress is part of the essential relation between demand and response, that is, it is part of the dimension of talk in the wider sense which includes also a 'talking' with things. Talk is also the fundamental sphere in which understanding becomes possible. (Ibid.)

These short excerpts offer an outline of what Heidegger means by language. It is more than the exchange of words. 'In the wider sense' it is the relation between demand and response, between address and answer. This is the relation between human beings and the world, between us and the phenomena that show themselves which includes 'things'. It is made possible by the human capacity of 'being open to' as well as to 'open up what *is*'.

Understanding

But in the special sense of the relation between human beings, language is an aspect of 'Being-with', that is, the ontological inevitability of 'Being-in-the-world-with-others'. As such it is closer to what we generally mean by 'talk', though even then it does not have to be verbal, as long as its aim is understanding. For Heidegger understanding is not intellectual comprehension but the openness towards the possibilities of whatever we meet, and this includes our own possibilities.

Understanding precedes knowledge. Let us take Heidegger's famous example of our use of a hammer: we have an understanding of what to do with it even if we do not know what it is made of, or what physical laws govern its function.

Communication

We see that language, as an aspect of Being-with is part of being human and that the use of words is only one way in which this ontological aspect of Being-with manifests itself. Heidegger distinguishes between ontological 'communication' – his word is 'Mitteilung' which implies 'sharing' – and special forms of it:

> ... the phenomenon of communication must be understood in an ontologically broad sense. 'Communication' in which we make statements, for example, giving information, is a special case of that communication which is grasped in principle existentially. Here the articulation of being-with-one-another understandingly is constituted. It brings about the 'sharing' of being attuned together and the understanding of being-with. (Heidegger, 1996, pp. 151–2)

Heidegger emphasizes that the communication does not start with words:

> Communication is never anything like a conveying of experiences, for example, opinions and wishes, from the inside of one subject to the inside of another. 'Mitda-sein' [Being-there-together] is essentially already manifest in attunement-with and understanding-with. Being-with is 'explicitly' *shared* in discourse, that is, it already *is*, – only unshared as something not grasped and appropriated. (Ibid.)

I have quoted Joan Stambaugh's translation, which I consider clearer and more accurate.

In order to comprehend the full meaning of this quotation something needs to be added to the description of Being-with as an 'attunement-with' as well as an 'understanding-with'. We shall return to the meaning of 'attunement' in a later chapter: the German word is 'Stimmung', and its translation is difficult as it applies both to the way an instrument is tuned and the mood we find ourselves in. At this point, it is perhaps enough to say that it describes what we might call the 'feeling-aspect' of a communication, how it affects us and how we affect it. Understanding and attunement cannot be separated, and in a 'with-world' it cannot be individualized – which inevitably strains our Western imagination (cf. Chapter 7).

Listening

That some understanding is immediate and does not need verbal expression is illustrated by Heidegger's distinction between phenomenological and psychological listening:

> Hearkening is phenomenally still more primordial than what is defined 'in the first instance' as 'hearing' in psychology – the sensing of tones and the perception of sounds. Hearkening . . . has the kind of Being of the hearing which understands. What we 'first' hear is never noises or complexes of sounds, but the creaking wagon, the motorcycle. We hear the column on the march, the woodpecker tapping, the fire crackling. (Heidegger, 1962, p. 207)

To this Heidegger adds surprisingly, but on reflection very accurately: 'It requires a very artificial and complicated frame of mind to "hear" a "pure noise"' (ibid.). From this point, Heidegger moves to the centre of his concern:

> The fact that motorcycles and wagons are what we proximally hear is the phenomenal evidence that in every case Dasein, as 'Being-in-the-world', already dwells *alongside* what is ready-to-hand within-the-world; it certainly does not dwell proximally alongside 'sensations' . . . Dasein, as essentially understanding, is proximally alongside what is understood. (Ibid.)

In other words: the world we share with others has meaning for us, 'speaks' to us, before words are used. This is also true in our discourse with others:

> Likewise, when we are explicitly hearing the discourse of others, we proximally understand what is said, or – to put it more exactly – we are already with him, in advance, alongside the entity which the discourse is about. On the other hand what we proximally hear is *not* what is expressed in the utterance. (Ibid.)
>
> (Stambaugh uses the word 'initially' for 'proximally', which is more intelligible. Heidegger's word is 'zunächst'.)

The most important term in this quotation is perhaps 'in advance' ('im Vorhinein'). This is a key to much of Heidegger's thinking and a correction of the popular notion of total personal freedom, which is based on a blurred interpretation of some of Sartre's sayings. In Heidegger's view, we always already bring a great deal into any situation – partly because our 'existence' implies inevitably certain aspects of Being (the 'existentials'), but also because we find ourselves in situations not initially chosen by us. However, the openness of the 'there' of our Dasein frees possibilities and frees us to choose or not choose them.

This view also shows the simultaneity of the three temporal dimensions (see Chapter 8); what is 'there' 'in advance', becomes the base for possibilities pointing towards a future. I believe the therapeutic process can also be seen in this way.

What we call 'language' is thus for Heidegger not restricted to the spoken word but is an 'existential'. As such it is perhaps more appropriately called 'communication' – the relation of beings sharing a 'with-world'.

The relevance of language to a therapy that relies to such an extent on a dialogue between therapist and the person in search of help is obvious. But Heidegger's view of language as an aspect of 'Being-with' adds another dimension to our understanding of this relevance.

Therapeutic relevance

1. First of all we need to remind ourselves that for Heidegger Being-with is an aspect of our being human. Being-with-others is not only a 'fact', it also implies a capacity, though as we have seen in the previous chapter it can be 'deficient' or suffer 'privation'.
2. Heidegger's view of language goes beyond the spoken word. It covers all the various manifestations of communication. Existential therapy ideally is open to what the total situation 'says' but will, of course, factually fall short of this as context is always unlimited.
3. This throws some light on the question of interpretation. Some people seem to think that existential therapy does not interpret – they are mistaken. Existential interpretation is not reductive, narrowing the context to the one true meaning which does not show itself. It is hermeneutic, broadening the known context so that a fuller understanding of the troubling phenomena is reached. The therapist can only assist in this clarification. The context is always the client's, and it is therefore his or her 'interpretation' which is likely to increase understanding.
4. There is a temptation to compare this process with that of 'making the unconscious conscious'. Such a comparison is encouraged by Heidegger's insistence that the phenomenon is not only what immediately shows itself, that in fact whatever shows itself arises from something that remains concealed. This is, of course, implied by the infinity of any context.

   The important difference between these two processes is, however, that hermeneutic interpretation does not replace what is known with what is concealed, but any disclosure extends what is already known, and thus the understanding of the total situation, though never fully reached, has been significantly increased.

   Heidegger discusses hermeneutic interpretation at a

number of places in *Being and Time*. He thought that we always bring already some understanding to whatever we wish to understand, and that every new insight is the ground for new insights – there is no end to this. His primary example for this is our understanding of Being which from the very beginning is of concern to us.

5. It is the therapist's task to aid this broadening of the client's understanding, and questions are, in my view, a way of doing this as long as they are truly questions and do not impose the therapist's own answer.

   Whatever way the therapist chooses, however, to assist this process s/he must not forget that the client needs to create her/his own context. Somebody else's interpretation, which is also often an explanation, may act as a foreign body within this creation and may invalidate the client's attempts at understanding.

6. In existential therapy everything a client says is meaningful, and it has to be received as meaningful. It means what it says and not something else – unless the client chooses it to do so. It may, of course, mean more than emerges at a particular time.

6 | Existence as Body-Mind

An enduring problem

The very moment we ask a question about the relation between body and mind, we have already entered the dualistic trap. It is as if we are trying to bring together two separate entities which, in fact, we have never seen apart. Who has ever met a mind without a body? Who has seen a living body without a mind?

The question about the relation between body and mind does usually assume that they are somehow connected, but it wishes also to know how one arises from the other. The need for a causal connection of separate entities seems to be part of our way of thinking. Neuroscientists wish to know: how does consciousness arise from matter? This has become known as the 'hard problem' of consciousness, and so far neuroscience has found it intractable. More specifically doctors and psychotherapists wish to know: how do mental conflicts generate physical symptoms? The answers to their questions have proved equally elusive. Freud, in his *Introductory Lectures* speaks at one point of 'the puzzling leap of the mental to the physical' (Freud, 1917, p. 258), and in his *Notes upon a Case of Obsessional Neurosis* he thinks that this leap 'can never be fully comprehensible to us' (Freud, 1909, p. 157).

Cartesian Dualism

Influenced by Cartesian thinking, psychotherapy is full of such 'leaps'. For as we have seen, there is not only a gap between body and mind, but also between one mind and another. Where the separation of mind and body is concerned Decartes is, once again, brutally straightforward: 'This "I" – that is the soul by which I am what I am – is entirely different from the body, and would not fail to be whatever it is even if the body did not exist' (Cottingham, 1993, p. 54).

If the separation between mind and body is so radical the explanation of their connection – which is too obvious to deny – becomes very difficult. Descartes himself found no satisfactory answer to this question. Some thinkers oppose a 'monism' to his 'dualism' denying reality to one or other of these entities. Thus 'idealists' deny reality to anything but mind, while 'materialists' believe only in the reality of matter. For 'monists', the problem of interaction, of course, does not arise, but the denial of an experience does not make it disappear.

Heidegger's view

What was Heidegger's view of the relation between body and mind? Did he see them as separate? How did he understand their interaction? Not much can be found about this in *Being and Time*. But we must not forget that *Being and Time* – in the words of his biographer – 'was a torso. It was planned in two parts, but not even the first was quite finished, even though Heidegger, under pressure, worked on it day and night' (Safranski, 1999, p. 171).

The 'pressure' was to write something substantial in order to keep his professional standing. It is generally agreed that those themes that he could not include in *Being and Time* found a place in his later work. Thus the body/mind question found its place in Heidegger's lectures in Switzerland. The fact that these were attended by a number of medically trained therapists certainly played a part in this.

Heidegger's definition of embodiment shows a way out of the dualism/monism dilemma: 'Embodiment is always an aspect of "Being-in-the-world". It always co-determines our "Being-in-the-world", our being-open, our partaking of world' (Heidegger, 1987, p. 126). Here body and mind participate equally in the act of existence. They are different aspects of Dasein's response to Being, different but not apart.

At the time Heidegger discussed embodiment in his seminars, he said, in a conversation with Boss, 'the term "psychosomatic medicine" tries to create a synthesis between two things which don't, in fact, exist' (ibid., p. 248). For there is, in fact, no independent 'psyche', nor is there an independent 'soma', and where there is no gap, there is no need for a bridge.

Heidegger illustrates his view very concretely by his comments on a lecture given by a Swiss physician to the Swiss Psychosomatic Society. In his lecture, a Professor Hegglin is reported to have said: 'Sadness cannot be measured – but the tears which are formed as a result of psychosomatic connections can be examined quantitatively in various ways' (ibid., p. 105). Heidegger comments: 'Tears cannot be measured, what you can measure is a fluid and its drops – tears can only be directly perceived. Where do tears belong? Are they something somatic or something psychic? They are neither' (ibid., p.106).

Heidegger then turns to the phenomenon of blushing. Here too you can, of course, measure the blood supply to the face. Heidegger asks again:

> But is blushing something somatic or something psychic? It is neither one nor the other. Phenomenologically, the reddening of our face when we feel ashamed can easily be distinguished from its redness when we have a fever, or when we enter a warm hut after having been out in the cold night on a mountain. All these forms of 'getting red' happen in our faces, but are nevertheless very different and can be distinguished immediately in our everyday being-with-and-for-each-other. (Ibid., p. 106)

Heidegger concludes: 'The situation itself shows us whether our fellow-human-being is ashamed or feels hot for some reason or other' (ibid.). This is, of course, the important point: soma and psyche, body and mind are both parts of a total situation, they are both aspects of the phenomenon we perceive, and to look at them separately misses the full meaning of what we meet. In this view, there is no causal interaction. But neither is there a monistic emphasis on the reality of only one of the two entities. Body and mind are two aspects of our being, each different in its manifestations. They are never apart but always responding simultaneously, though often with different intensity, to whatever situation they find themselves in.

The example of stress

In his *Zollikon Seminars*, Heidegger explores at some length a situation that shows clearly the co-response of body and mind – the situation of 'stress' (cf. Chapter 5, p. 43). He says:

> Stress means demands, a burden, and even easing a burden can be stressful. Why is it that a certain amount of stress is life-preserving? This is rooted in our ekstatic being. It is a fundamental structure of being human. In it there is grounded the openness which enables us to be addressed by whatever we are not ourselves. Without being addressed in this way, we could not exist.
> As far as this necessary ability to be addressed is concerned, the 'burden' of it is what preserves life. As long as we think of a human being as a worldless 'I', we cannot understand the vital necessity of this burden of stress. If stress is understood in this way it is an aspect of the essence of ek-sisting beings. (Ibid., p. 180)

Here stress is not just seen as threatening and potentially traumatic, something that overwhelms the emotional and physical aspects of being human. It arises from the very capacity of being open to what addresses us, what speaks to us and requires our answer – a capacity which Heidegger sees as the essence of human 'ek-sistence', our ability to 'stand out', to go beyond ourselves.

In this analysis, stress is not seen, as it frequently is, as the physical response to a mental injury, but as the existential response to a demand of Being. If we were not open to it, it could not overwhelm us. It is not a 'pathological' event as such.

Two aspects of Being

In one of his conversations with Boss, Heidegger emphasizes the part our bodily being plays in our capacity to answer what addresses us 'from the openness of the world' (ibid., p. 292).

> Whatever we call our bodiliness – including the last muscle fibre and the most hidden hormone molecule – is an essential aspect of our existence. It is fundamentally not lifeless matter but the realm of an unobjectifiable invisible capacity to perceive the meaning of what we encounter. Our Dasein is basically this capacity of perception. (Ibid., p. 293)

At this point Heidegger is very close to Merleau-Ponty's views on the 'task' of the body as discussed in his *Phenomenology of Perception* (1962). Heidegger clearly distinguishes between the living and the dead body: 'In dying the bodily realm transfers itself into the state of being of a lifeless thing, into a corpse' (ibid.). (The German language has different words for the living and the dead body.)

In Heidegger's view, our physical aspects show what we existentially are: 'We do not perceive beings because we have eyes – we can only have eyes because we are fundamentally perceiving beings' (ibid.).

Therapeutic relevance

1. If we see the body and mind as different aspects of the total situation of Being, they are always both affected whenever

changes in this situation lead to what we may call 'disturbances'. Such changes may manifest themselves more forcibly in the bodily than in the mental sphere, or may be perceived more clearly in it – and vice versa – but both realms are aspects of the same phenomenon, and both need attention and understanding.

2. What we call 'psychosomatic symptoms' – which are usually seen as the physical manifestations of unexpressed feelings or emotional conflicts – can perhaps be better understood as a total response to a total situation which simultaneously affects our physical and non-physical being. Thus a state of anxiety does not *cause* our palms to sweat and our heart to race, but these physical signs *are* as much our state of anxiety as our anxious thoughts. The question then is: What makes us experience, say, the physical signs much more (or less) clearly than the anxious thoughts? (The word anxiety does contain, of course, a reference to physical manifestations!) The exploration of the total situation may help us to understand this.
3. Monistic theories tend to confuse therapy. Thus a theory that assumes that all 'mental' changes are due to 'physical' imbalance (which is the view of many psychiatrists) denies reality to the mind. Similarly, the assumption that 'physical' means should not be used in our approach to 'mental' disturbances (which is the view of many psychotherapists) denies reality to the body.
4. The holistic view of existential phenomenology questions these assumptions. If the body and mind are, in fact, not separate, there is no reason why a therapeutic approach needs to be either physical or non-physical. The choice needs to be based on other criteria, keeping the total situation in view. All choices involve, of course, risks. Some physical approaches have proved unsuitable and even dangerous. I am certain that this can equally be said of some non-physical approaches, though this may be more difficult to show.

5. Also, let us not forget that there are no approaches that are purely physical – certainly not as long as living, thinking and feeling human beings are involved. Nor are there any which are purely non-physical – clients and therapist are not disembodied minds, they have faces and voices. As I said when I embarked on this theme – as soon as we talk about the 'physical' and the 'non-physical', we tend to be caught in the trap of dualism.

7 Existence's 'Attunement'

Problems of translation

Heidegger's thinking about the aspect of our existence that we generally call 'emotions' has, on the whole, been neglected. The main problem is, once again, the difficulty of translating the words Heidegger uses to convey his understanding of this area. The two words that Heidegger uses are 'Befindlichkeit' and 'Stimmung'. They are very telling words in the original German. 'Befindlichkeit' describes literally how we find ourselves and 'Stimmung' refers to the way we are 'tuned'. Macquarrie translates 'Befindlichkeit' as 'state-of-mind' and 'Stimmung' as 'mood'.

'State-of-mind' is generally found to be inadequate because as Polt puts it: 'after all Heidegger consistently tries to avoid giving the impression that Dasein exists inside a subjective sphere, such as a mind' (Polt, 1999, p. 65). Polt opts for Stambaugh's choice of 'attunement'. But he mentions a number of other translations which taken together convey the wide range of meaning the word covers: 'Disposition would be another good way to render "Befindlichkeit" because it helps us to think of our mood as what "positions" us in the world, giving us an orientation. Others have tried "situatedness", "affectedness", "so-foundness"' (ibid.).

Feeling instead of mood

'Mood' for 'Stimmung' has been more generally accepted and is also Polt's choice. I would like to take the liberty of using the word 'feeling' for 'Stimmung'. This is, of course, not an adequate translation either – the implication of 'sound' is missing, indicated by 'Stimme', which means voice.

However, 'feeling' meant originally a 'sense of touch', both physically and emotionally, thus both bringing and receiving something, not just reactive but interactive, and, as we shall see, also disclosive.

Heidegger expressed the relation between what I shall now call 'attunement' and 'feeling' quite clearly: 'What we indicate *ontologically* by the term "attunement" is *ontically* the most familiar and everyday sort of thing; our "feeling"' (Heidegger, 1962, p. 172).

From this perspective, feelings are part of a situation and contribute to it and they cannot be seen as attaching themselves to this or that event. Feelings belong to the 'Da' of 'Sein', to the 'there of Being'. In Heidegger's words (having replaced 'mood' with 'feeling'): 'A "feeling" assails us. It comes neither from "outside" nor from "inside", but arises out of Being-in-the-world, as a way of such Being' (ibid., p. 176).

Disclosive feelings

Feelings are not only reactive but they are also disclosive. As Polt puts it: 'they show us things in a more fundamental way than theoretical propositions ever can' (Polt, 1999, p. 66). Polt gives us two examples. He refers to Heidegger's attempt 'to define the fearsome phenomenally in its fearsomeness' (Heidegger, 1962, p. 179). Heidegger asks: 'What do we encounter in fearing that belongs to the fearsome as such?' (ibid.). And his answer is entirely untheoretical: 'That in the face of which we fear can be characterized as threatening' (ibid.). Here experience takes the place of explanation.

Polt's other example comes from one of Heidegger's earliest works. Heidegger says there: 'We are in the habit of saying that love is blind (but) love really gives us sight' (Heidegger, 1985, p. 296).

Damasio's view

In Western thinking, reason and feelings have been considered predominantly as separate functions: reason is seen as active and sensible, with the task of mastering reactive and irrational feelings. Heidegger views this as another dualism to be challenged: reason and feelings are both aspects of existence and cannot be separated.

It is noteworthy that even in neuroscience the separation between rationality and feelings is now questioned. In his introduction to his book *Descartes' Error* the eminent neurologist Antonio R. Damasio writes:

> I began writing this book to propose that reason may not be as pure as most of us think it is or wish it were and that emotions and feelings may not be intruders in the bastion of reason at all. They may be enmeshed in its networks, for worse and for better. (Damasio, 1994, p. xiv)

More importantly, Damasio reaches the conclusion that: 'contrary to traditional scientific opinion, feelings are just as cognitive as percepts' (ibid., p. xvii). This comes quite close to Heidegger's view that 'Stimmung' is disclosive.

Therapeutic relevance

1. Feelings cannot be 'split off' from the situation in which they occur. They cannot be isolated or 'repressed', and return later attached to events to which they did not originally belong. An unexpressed anger, for instance, is an unexpressed anger, no more, no less. It is not an anger

clamouring for expression and excluded from it. The fact that it is unexpressed is part of what it is.

2. Feelings cannot be revived in their original purity because they are part of a context that cannot be recreated. The pain of the hurt child belongs in the context of childhood and cannot be re-experienced by the adult. However, the fact that it can be remembered in a new adult context may help towards a new response and open the trap in which it caught us. In this sense, the memory of the adult's past becomes therapeutic.
3. There is no purely cognitive approach to problems. The superiority of rationality, an important trait in Western thinking, cannot be maintained. Neither can be, of course, a superiority of feeling. The price we pay for an acceptance of the multidimensionality of experience is to give up the emphasis on one part of it.

8 | Existence as Temporality

What is time?

Our exploration of time has gone the way of much of Western thinking. In order to be able to control our experiences, we tend to take them apart and reduce them to 'components'. Thus we divided our experience of time into the dimensions of past, present and future; then we saw it as a series of 'nows'; finally we imagined these 'nows' to be of equal duration so we numbered and counted them. Next we could introduce a division of this sequence into hours, minutes and seconds. We developed a most useful spatial representation of time that helped us to construct the timetables that we find so necessary for everyday living. But do we know any more about the nature of time?

It is surprisingly difficult to say what time is. St Augustine admitted that he knew what time was as long as nobody asked him about it. In this he was quite near to Heidegger for whom time remained a question which he attempts to answer in a number of different ways. On the other hand, Aristotle saw time as a sequence of 'nows': each 'now' had its 'before' and 'after', and this helped us to understand the nature of motion.

With Aristotle we are already in the realm of counting and measuring, the scientific way of 'using' time. Heidegger, however, did not think we could define time by measuring it. 'We can only measure time, if we already have such a thing as time' (Heidegger, 1987, p. 53). Measuring time tells us nothing about time itself, except that it is measurable.

A phenomenology of time

The phenomenological approach does not think you can 'explain' time, it is an experience, a phenomenon in the sense in which Heidegger describes phenomena: 'What phenomena . . . demand is only that we perceive them and accept how they show themselves' (ibid., p. 80).

Talking to practitioners and students of psychiatry in Switzerland in 1965, Heidegger illustrated this phenomenological approach very clearly and showed how much can be learned about the nature of time by describing how we experience it:

> Past, future and present we call dimensions of time . . . All three dimensions are equally original, for there is none without the other two, and thus all three are equally open to us, though not uniformly so. At times, one dimension dominates and becomes the one that engages and perhaps imprisons us. But this does not mean that other dimensions have disappeared, they are only modified. (Ibid., p. 61)

And again, even nearer to actual experience:

> Having time for something, I am directed towards a 'what-for', towards what is to be done, what is coming. I am awaiting it but in a way that I still dwell in what is present, and in addition I also retain (whether I wish to or not) what occupied me just now and before. (Ibid., p. 84)

What these pronouncements emphasize is the experience of time's three-dimensionality. There is no linear move from past via present to future, as every present moment still contains the past it left behind while already pointing towards a future. Our very sentences receive their meaning from what has already been said and what still remains to be said. Thus time is not a thread but a web which refers simultaneously to what is, what has been and what is to be.

Husserl on time

Heidegger's phenomenology of time, as has been pointed out by Robert J. Dostal, was developed within the framework of Husserl's phenomenological method. Husserl had expressed his ideas about time in lectures from 1905 on, and they appeared in 1928 as a book under the title *The Phenomenology of Internal Time Consciousness*. Though Husserl and Heidegger had substantial disagreements on many aspects of phenomenology, it appears that Heidegger was strongly indebted to Husserl's view of time.

Husserl shelved what he called 'objective time' and inquired into the constitution of time within experience. He also reached the notion of three-dimensionality. Dostal sums up his conclusions:

> Any present moment . . . has what he calls 'retentive' and 'protentive' aspects. In other words, any moment is what it is in virtue of what it retains from the past (retention) and what it anticipates from the future (protention). Every present moment carries these two aspects as essential to its being what it is as present. (Dostal, 1993, p. 146)

Though it seems likely that Heidegger, the much younger man who was still at school when Husserl started to lecture on time, was influenced by his view on it, it is, of course, possible that he came to similar conclusions by using the phenomenological method when exploring the experience. This method he had indeed learned from Husserl.

Heidegger's existential dimensions

What is more important is that Heidegger added an existential dimension to the phenomenological one, and thus opened up new areas of understanding. In order to comprehend the existential dimension of Heidegger's view of time, we need to remember how Heidegger uses the word 'existential'. As we have seen, he turns to its original meaning – its derivation from the Latin 'ex-sistere' (to stand out). To Heidegger it describes the specific ability of human beings to go beyond, to 'transcend' their immediate situation. To have a present, which contains the past and is pointing towards a future, is an illustration of this capacity that is, in Heidegger's thinking, not shared by other beings. Animals and plants do not 'exist', they simply 'are'. It is an aspect of being human that we are capable of being aware of our existence and what it implies, and that it is of concern to us.

Existential time

Existential phenomenology does not try to define what time is as such. It sees time as an aspect of our experience of existence. What time might mean or be if we did not live it we cannot know. Time is not something 'within' which our life unfolds, though this is often how it is seen. Heidegger warns us that talking about living 'in time' implies the particular difficulty of assuming 'that time is a kind of container of space' (Heidegger, 1987, p. 57). He suggests 'that there is clearly something like a necessary interdependence of time and human beings' (ibid., p. 48).

Time matters to us, as Heidegger emphasizes in his thinking about 'having time':

> We started with our everyday experience of time from what we mean when we talk of 'having time', 'having no time', 'to take time', 'to give up time', 'to waste time'. All this shows in some way our relation to time, but it clearly depends on the fact that we are already in possession of time, that it is granted to us so that we can use it in one way or another. And particularly when we have no time, the time granted to us oppresses us. Time affects us. Time concerns us. (Ibid., p. 77)

Our experience of time reaches from 'unchosen' limitations to the chosen realization of our possibilities, whereby the choice is carried by our free responses. Another way of describing this process is to call it our history.

Human beings can thus be seen not so much to live *in* time as to be living it. At every moment, the past is the soil from which we are already stretching out towards a future.

Therapeutic relevance

What relevance has this view of time to a psychotherapy informed by existential phenomenology? Time does, of course, play an important part in any kind of therapy: you see a client at a certain time, for a certain duration, once or a number of times during the week. But this is essentially measured time, indispensable for practical reasons, a means of fixing and co-ordinating time rather than telling us something about the nature of time itself. What is the relevance of existential time to psychotherapy?

1. One hour is as long as any other – but it is experienced as long, short, or long at first, short afterwards and so on by different people at different times. Here a gap opens up between what we call 'clock-time' and 'lived time'.
2. Some therapies focus on what is called the 'here-and-now', trying to stay by what is going on during the session, and excluding what has happened before or may happen afterwards – outside the actual therapy, so to speak – in an attempt to create a pure present. The aim is an experience uncontaminated by past events or future expectations. In the light of a phenomenological view of time as three-dimensional this is not possible. The present, as both Husserl and Heidegger emphasize, contains at any moment the past and points to the future.
3. I do not say that past experiences or the anticipation of what is to come *cause* aspects of our present experience.

Causality is essentially linear, and, as we have seen, time is not a thread but a web in which all our experiences find their place and influence each other. Our perception of past events is as much affected by where we find ourselves at present as by what we expect or desire to happen in the future.

Existential psychotherapy can therefore do without the construction of an 'Unconscious' – a psychological location which serves to house and hide earlier events and feelings until they find an opportunity to emerge again. When the past is always an aspect of the present, it is more a question of whether we can face it or prefer to walk away. The experience of the interconnection between past and present is perhaps obscured by an explanatory mechanism that distances it. This is why existential therapists give priority to the phenomena, what 'meets the eye', so to speak, over explanations.

4. While the past has an important place in most kinds of psychotherapy, the future is, on the whole, neglected. This is to some extent an aspect of a causal approach to exploration where we are mainly concerned with what went before, its origin. But in fact the future is inevitably crucial in the process of psychotherapy as soon as we consider its aim. But all aims are rooted in what already is.

   The aim of psychotherapy is difficult to describe – different approaches have different aims and different criteria of progress. But most seem to aim at change of one kind or another. And change implies a move towards a future. We frequently come up against a situation so strongly dominated by the past that change seems impossible. Thus it becomes important to be able to distinguish what is unchangeable from what can be changed. There are two different kinds of 'givens' – the givens of circumstance, and the givens of existence itself. The givens of circumstance are different for each of us – we do not choose our parents, the country of our birth, its social structure, its language, laws and customs. We have already met the givens of existence – what Heidegger calls the 'existentials' – aspects of being which are shared by all human beings: our mortality, our Being-in-a-world, our Being-with-others, our Being-in-a-body. These givens we have not chosen either. But while givens themselves are beyond change, our responses to them can be changed or modified. Here is the place for freedom and for change.

The possibility of a free response to their 'givens' is unlikely to be within the reach of many of our clients' minds when they first come to see us. They tend to be deeply caught in the trap of their 'givens', expecting us to release them from it.

Existential approaches focus on the experience that while the 'givens' are unchangeable, our responses are not fixed. Whatever our parents, say, have done or failed to do may be unalterable. But these past events are now part of a different present with different possibilities, and as meaning arises from context, they may now have a different meaning. New choices open up which may or may not be made. But even if a new direction is not taken, *this* can be experienced as a new choice.

A multidimensional view of time grants us an area of freedom, which a predetermined chain of 'nows' withholds from us.

9 | The Priority of the Phenomena

What is phenomenology

What is a phenomenon? In a recent dictionary of philosophy it is defined as 'a thing (a quality, a relation, a state of affairs, an event, etc.) as it appears to us, as it is perceived'. A comment is added to this definition: 'Phenomena, appearances, data are implicitly contrasted with the way things really are. This contrast gives rise to one of the fundamental problems of philosophy: whether or how far we can have knowledge of the way things really are' (Mautner, 1996, p. 421).

Phenomenology is defined in the same dictionary as:

> the philosophical method and movement that had its origin in the work of Edward Husserl (1859–1938). It is the attempt to describe our experience directly, as it is, separately from its origin and development, independent of the causal explanations that historians, sociologists and psychologists might give. Subsequently, Heidegger, Sartre and Merleau-Ponty pursued and continued to refine the phenomenological method, while by no means accepting Husserl's conclusions. (Ibid.)

This is an admirable, straightforward and lucid definition, much needed if we wish to understand the various forms in which phenomena and phenomenology concretely manifest themselves.

Differences between Husserl and Heidegger

We have already met the difference between Husserl and Heidegger's phenomenology and we shall meet it again. This is the nature of our exploration into the relevance of certain Heideggerian notions to the practice of psychotherapy. It will repeatedly introduce the same themes in different contexts, thus broadening and clarifying their meaning, rather than presenting a unified continuous argument.

We have seen that Husserl by 'stripping away the variants of experience' (Spinelli, 1989, p. 16) was trying to explore the essence of this experience. The method for doing this was the suspension, the 'bracketing' of 'the natural standpoint', eventually even going beyond the experiencing ego. We could say this suspension involved bracketing the phenomena of the world.

But for Heidegger, who saw human Being as 'Being-in-the-world', such 'stripping away' was not possible even experimentally. There could be no human being without world, no world without human being – no essence without existence: 'the essence of Dasein lies in its existence' (Heidegger, 1962, p. 67).

Heidegger was not alone in questioning Husserl's 'epochē'. Robert Solomon puts it thus:

> A man is not a detachable consciousness who can abstract himself from the world around him ... The most important link among existential phenomenologists ... is their insistence that it is not possible to abstract oneself from involvement in the world. One cannot 'bracket' existence, as the epochē requires; our existence and the existence of the world around us are given together as the starting point of all phenomenological description. (Solomon, 1987, p. 179)

Phenomenological rules

What about those phenomenological 'rules' or 'steps' that Spinelli describes and which are often recommended as a guide for the existential therapist? They do not, in my view, follow Husserl; they do not exclude the world but on the contrary open it up. 'The Rule of Epochē' asks us to set aside biases and prejudices and 'urges us to impose an "openness" on our immediate experience' (Spinelli, 1989, p. 17). This seems to echo Heidegger's 'existence as Da-sein opening up a sphere where the sense of what is given can be perceived' (Heidegger, 1987, p. 4).

The second rule, 'The Rule of Description', is summed up as 'Describe, don't explain' – explanation is seen as a limitation. It has no place in Heidegger's hermeneutics either, which knows no final answers.

Finally, 'The Rule of Horizontalization', 'urges us to avoid placing any hierarchies of significance or importance upon the items of our descriptions' (ibid., p. 18). To do this would, of course, be the first step on the way to an explanation and an 'objectification' of the experience. Here is no Husserlian 'bracketing' but a suspension of pre-judgement.

In my view, it was Heidegger who turned Husserl's method into an existential phenomenology where interpretation is hermeneutic, that is, continuous and never final, and where the phenomena are understood not explained.

Freud's view

Freud, in his *Introductory Lectures*, proposed a very different view:

> We seek not merely to describe and to classify phenomena, but to understand them as signs of an inter-play of forces in the mind, as a manifestation of purposeful intentions working concurrently or in mutual opposition. We are concerned with a dynamic view of

> mental phenomena. In our view the phenomena that are perceived must yield in importance to trends which are only hypothetical. (Freud, 1916, p. 67)

There can be no clearer adoption of a non-phenomenological view. Phenomena have no priority; they are seen as 'signs' of processes within the mind, even though these are admitted to be 'trends, which are only hypothetical'. This passage sums up the basic distinction between a psychodynamic and an existential-phenomenological approach.

Heidegger's view

Heidegger's definition of phenomenology seems clear and simple: 'phenomenology means . . . to let that which shows itself be seen from itself in the very way in which it shows itself from itself' (Heidegger, 1962, p. 58). To this he adds a later point: 'To have a science "of" phenomena means to grasp its object in such a way that everything about them which is up for discussion must be treated by exhibiting it directly and demonstrating it directly' (ibid., p. 59).

But soon we come to realize that Heidegger's definition is not so clear and simple after all. Phenomena are for him not just what meets the external eye, they have a hidden aspect:

> What is it that phenomenology is to 'let us see'? . . . What is it that by its very essence is *necessarily* the theme whenever we exhibit something *explicitly*? Manifestly it is something that for the most part does *not* show itself at all: it is something that lies *hidden* . . . but at the same time is something that belongs to what thus shows itself, and it belongs to it so essentially as to constitute its meaning and its ground. Yet that which remains *hidden* in an egregious sense, or which relapses and gets *covered up* again, or which shows itself only 'in disguise', is not just this entity or that, but rather the Being of entities. (Ibid., p. 59)

What is this hidden aspect of the phenomenon? It is its 'Being' as such, always there, always elusive. It is easily forgotten, but without it there would be nothing.

We are already familiar with the temptation of a comparison between this hidden aspect and Freud's unconscious meaning of what we say and do. Here I only wish to point out once more that the discovery of what is 'hidden' does not take the place of what has already been seen but extends and clarifies it without ever reaching a final answer.

The priority of the phenomena, an openness to what shows itself even if part of it is still hidden, is one of Heidegger's most important convictions. It is this that he calls 'understanding' and he sees it as a central capacity of human existence.

Polt's commentary is illuminating here:

> Heidegger holds that although most entities are independent of us, their Being is not ... Being is necessarily linked to our understanding, because it is the difference that entities make to us. Being is what allows us to encounter every entity. (Polt, 1999, p. 41)

In the light of Heidegger's concern with Dasein's understanding of Being, the impression given by some writers that he gave up his interest in phenomenology in the later part of his life seems strange. In the *Zollikon Seminars* Heidegger stresses frequently both the difficulty and necessity of focusing on the phenomena. But it is true that at this point in his life he turned more specifically to the way in which he formulated his questions at the beginning in *Being and Time*.

Heidegger and science

For instance, after talking in the *Zollikon Seminars* about the phenomena of blushing and sadness (cf. pp. 53f.), Heidegger returned to the difficulty of 'making certain phenomena visible'. He added:

> It is important to let these phenomena simply stand in the way as they first came into view, without attempting to retrace their origin. In other words, we need to refuse any possibility of reducing them to something else. Instead we need to examine to what extent these phenomena as they are, are already sufficiently defined and contain in themselves references to other phenomena to which they essentially belong. (Heidegger, 1987, p. 111)

This approach is, of course, the opposite of what we have come to call 'scientific'. Heidegger has often been accused of being hostile to the sciences, and in the *Zollikon Seminars* he defends himself against such accusations, adding at the same time another aspect of his view of phenomenology:

> Our considerations should by no means be seen as hostile to science. Science is in no way refuted. It is only its absolute demand to be the only measure of all that is true which is rejected as presumptuous. To oppose this unacceptable demand it seems necessary to me to call our very different method an 'engagement with what we encounter' (and of which we are always already a part). An aspect of phenomenology is, so to speak, the wish not to avoid this engagement. (Ibid., p. 143)

Polt offers a lucid summary of Heidegger's view of phenomenology and underlines its existential character which distinguishes it from Husserl's:

> Heidegger's phenomenological ontology is hermeneutical: that is, it interprets Being as Dasein, and it examines the process of interpretation itself. Interpretation is the act of developing one's understanding of something . . .
>
> In fact, an interpretation is always subject to revision and elaboration. We have seen that Heidegger himself follows a 'spiral' structure in which he continually reinterprets the phenomena. There is no point at which we can safely conclude this process of interpretation and reach a perfect, definitive account of things . . .

> Thanks largely to Heidegger, hermeneutics has gained wide acceptance as an approach to philosophy in general. Many thinkers now view knowledge not as a static set of correct propositions, but as a continuing search for better interpretation. (Polt, 1999, p. 41)

Therapeutic relevance

1. We have already stressed the special nature of a hermeneutic interpretation that, as Polt puts it, is 'always subject to revision and elaboration' and 'that there is no point at which we can safely conclude this process'. An existential-phenomenological therapist will employ this type of interpretation. This is, of course, very different from the psychoanalytic approach that finds an answer to the question: what does this mean? And finds it in a 'perfect, definitive' form through the exploration of a place in the psyche called the 'unconscious'.
2. Our dictionary definition of 'phenomenon' touched on the question of reality – are 'phenomena' only the appearance of things, and how far do we ever penetrate to what is 'real'?

   For Heidegger this is not a meaningful question. 'The question of whether there is a world at all and whether its Being can be proved, makes no sense if it is raised by Dasein as Being-in-the-world; and who else could raise it?' (Heidegger, 1962, pp. 246–7)

   In other words, the question can only be asked when we see ourselves as separate from the world – otherwise it would question our own reality. Thus the reality of phenomena is not in doubt. They are what they show, and what more is discovered of them illuminates their being.
3. Phenomenological interpretation of symptoms, dreams and strange behaviour does not, therefore, mean discovering the 'true' or 'real' meaning behind what shows itself. Rather it furthers the process of understanding as much of the

meaning of the phenomenon as is possible at the time. It is this process that Heidegger calls hermeneutical, and continuous reinterpretation is part of it.

4. Similarly, the therapeutic situation is what it shows: two people concerned with the story of one of them. There is no 'deeper reality' behind it. Those features that are called 'transference' are the revival of past experience as an aspect of present reality.

10 Being and Beings

The ontological difference

When we retraced, in an opening chapter, Heidegger's 'Way to Psychotherapy' we found that his central concern with Being as such, the very fact that there is something rather than nothing, led him to explore the Being of human beings. For they were not only concerned with being one thing or another, being tall or short, loving or hating, men or women, shopkeepers or lawyers, but also – even if less often and less clearly – with Being as such. The concern with Being as such leads inevitably to the difference between there being something and there being nothing and thus, of course, also to our own mortality.

It was the exploration of this concern that brought into Heidegger's view certain phenomena that also engaged the interest of psychotherapists – phenomena like anxiety, embodiment, language, the relation of people with each other. In this way a connection opened up between Heidegger's somewhat abstract interest in Being as such, and the concrete misapprehensions and disturbances which led human beings to seek the help of psychotherapists.

Heidegger distinguishes between the two meanings of 'is' in the sentences 'John is' and 'John is a student'. In the first sentence, the 'is' indicates John's 'Being' which is the ground of whatever the 'is' in the second sentence describes – here John 'is' a particular 'being', a student.

Heidegger calls whatever belongs to 'Being' as such 'ontological', and whatever describes 'beings' as 'ontic'. The distinction between the two is the 'ontological difference'.

Heidegger expounds on this difference in the *Zollikon Seminars*:

> There are two kinds of phenomena:
>
> a) Perceivable phenomena ('beings' = ontic phenomena, e.g. the table).
>
> b) Not sensually perceivable phenomena, e.g. the existence of something = ontological phenomena …
>
> Before we can perceive a table, we must have a sense of something like 'Anwesen' (presence, thereness, Being). Ontological phenomena have, in fact, priority, but take second place in our thinking and perception. (Heidegger, 1987, p. 7)

We see in this quotation that things like tables also have Being which enables us to perceive what they are, for instance, wooden or brown. This Being, however, we cannot perceive. Like human beings they have an ontological and an ontic aspect.

Human and non-human beings

Human beings are, however, different from things like tables in that they have an awareness of their own Being and the Being of other human beings. Tables have no such awareness.

This special concern that only human beings have for Being, Heidegger describes in the following way: 'Das Dasein ist Seiendes, dem es in seinem Sein um dieses selbst geht.' This is a crucial sentence but very difficult to translate. Literally it says: 'There-being is being whose concern, in its Being, is this very Being itself.' Macquarrie's translation 'Dasein is an entity for which, in its Being, that Being is an issue' (Heidegger, 1962, p. 236) loses weight by the weak word 'issue'. Stambaugh's translation is more appropriate: 'Da-sein is a being which is concerned in its being about that being' (Heidegger, 1996, p. 179). This rendering is marred by her decision not to distinguish the ontological *Be*ing from the ontic *be*ing. (In German, we can see, we have two different words.)

What is Dasein's 'concern'? In Heidegger's thinking, Dasein is always, however dimly, concerned for its 'ownmost potentiality-for-Being. This potentiality is that for the sake of which any Dasein is as it is. In each case Dasein has already compared itself, in its Being, with a possibility of itself' (Heidegger, 1962, p. 236).

We can now see why Heidegger thinks of human beings as being radically different from other beings. They are pregnant with possibility, though they are not always aware of it, and at times tend to forget it altogether.

Another difference between human beings and other beings is their potential awareness of 'existentials' – those universal aspects of Being which we have frequently met throughout our various explorations. They are rooted in common human experience – experiential universals, so to speak, rather than conceptual ones. Heidegger has not given us a complete list of them but refers to them whenever he turns to ontological aspects of phenomena.

For instance, anxiety is experienced by all of us. 'Being-in-the-world itself is that in the face of which anxiety is anxious' (ibid., p. 234). Anxiety is an aspect of Being, it is ontological. It is the ground on which a spectrum of fears, each specific to the individual human being, reveals itself – fears are ontic.

Relation between the ontic and the ontological

Heidegger stressed the relation between the ontic and the ontological. 'There are some things which every ontical understanding "includes", even if these are only pre-ontological – that is to say, not conceived theoretically or thematically' (ibid., p. 360). The ontological is not hidden *behind* the ontic: it is 'included' in it, and our understanding has access to it though we may not be able to articulate it. This may be relevant for therapy, as we shall see.

Non-human beings also have Being, are also 'ontological' but they lack existence. Non-human beings do not 'stand out' of their selves and show concern for their Being. Human beings, on the other hand, are defined by their existentiality, by their potential awareness of the existentials, which are aspects of Being as such. 'These are to be sharply distinguished from what we call "categories" – characteristics of Being for entities whose character is not that of Dasein' (Heidegger, 1962, p. 70). Such 'categories' of non-human beings are, for instance, quality and quantity. Heidegger illustrates the difference between ontological and ontic phenomena shown by non-human beings to Medard Boss in a hand-written text which comments on the manuscript of a book Boss was writing at the time:

> The ontological phenomena cannot be seen as immediately as the ontic ones. These – like colour, weight etc. – are also pre-determined as 'quality'. Colour is a quality – this is, however, neither coloured nor heavy, nor thick or long. It is not ontically determined but ontologically. (Heidegger, 1987, p. 281)

This quotation takes us back to Heidegger's distinction between ontological and ontic phenomena that opened this chapter. There he proposed the 'ontological difference' (taking the table as an example) without paying special attention to the existentiality of a human being, that is, Dasein. But when we now turn to the relevance of 'ontological difference' to therapy, human existentiality is, of course, crucial.

Therapeutic relevance

1. Heidegger makes a radical distinction between human and non-human beings. Both are ontologically determined, that is, they are related to Being. But for human beings there are aspects of Being which are universally experienced – they

are the 'existentials'. They are 'given', and we cannot choose them. We have, however, the freedom to choose our response to them.

2. Our response to ontological 'givens' is ontic. There is a wide spectrum of ontic responses to ontological givens. It is these responses that we encounter as therapists. Heidegger, in addressing his students, emphasized that these ontic phenomena need to be taken seriously and should not be hastily interpreted ontologically:

   > It is decisive that whatever phenomena appear in the relation between analysand and analyst are expressed as belonging to the actual patient, and in a language that brings out their phenomenal content. They should not be subordinated to an all-inclusive existential. (Ibid., p. 162)

   Not many of Heidegger's comments touch so directly on the practice of existential therapy. His suggestion here is of great importance: it warns us not to jump to ontological conclusions that the ontic phenomena do not by themselves disclose. Though ontological anxiety may play its part in the development of a phobia or a panic attack, a direct ontological interpretation would be as reductive as any psychoanalytic reading.

3. On the other hand, Heidegger has also said that a kind of 'pre-ontological' understanding is 'included' in 'every ontical understanding' (Heidegger, 1962, p. 360) and there is no reason why the therapist should refrain from helping the client to discover this. Such a discovery – which in Heidegger's view is always a kind of 're-covery' – can lead to a change of response and thus to a change of the total situation.

11 | The Question of Authenticity

What is authenticity?

Approaching the theme of authenticity, we immediately raise a cluster of questions: What do we mean by it? What did Heidegger mean by it? Does his meaning correspond with ours? Can it be an aim of human development as some existential therapists propose? Would this be what Heidegger had in mind or advocated?

Heidegger does, in fact, distinguish a 'Man-selbst' from an 'eigentlichen . . . Selbst'. This distinction is rendered in Macquarrie's translation in the following way:

> The self of everyday Dasein is the *'they-self'*, which we distinguish from the *authentic Self* – that is, from the Self which has been taken hold of in its own way ... As they-self the particular Dasein has been dispersed into the 'they', and must first find itself. (Heidegger, 1962, p. 167)

This translation is, however, to some extent misleading. A literal translation of Heidegger's text would have to present the 'they-self' as a 'one-self', as the German 'man' has the meaning we would give 'one' in sentences like: 'one agrees' or 'one does not do this'. When we refer to 'they', we exclude ourselves while Heidegger includes us in the 'one'.

The more problematic translation, however, is the rendering

of 'eigentlich' as 'authentic'. If 'authentic' would have been the right word for Heidegger, he might have used the German 'authentisch', which means more or less what it means in English. But in both languages it has acquired some associations that tend to obscure what Heidegger wanted to say. Whether he just did not think of it, or avoided it, it was clearly not the 'right word' for him.

On the other hand, it has to be admitted that it is very difficult to find a suitable translation for 'eigentlich' and convey the sense Heidegger seems to have had in mind. Joan Stambaugh also uses 'authentic'.

Let us compare the meaning of 'authentic' with the way Heidegger uses the word he has chosen – 'eigentlich'. Initially 'authenticity' seems to have been an attribute of a thing when it was the original itself and not a copy, 'legally valid' and 'first-hand' as the Oxford Concise Dictionary has it – in one word: genuine. A thing was authentic when it was neither a copy nor a forgery. And something can only be a copy or a forgery when we know (or know of) an original that it pretends to be. It seems to me questionable whether the term could ever be attributed meaningfully to a human being.

Heidegger's original concept

The word Heidegger uses and which has been translated as 'authentic' is 'eigentlich'.

This derives from 'eigen' which means 'own'. It is also part of the German word 'Eigenschaft' (quality) as well as the word 'Eigentum' (possession).

It is a very common word in colloquial German, but Heidegger, in applying it to 'self', gives it a very specific meaning. In the passage I quoted, Macquarrie translates Heidegger's definition as 'the self that has been taken hold of in its own way'. I prefer Stambaugh's rendering: 'the self which has explicitly grasped itself' (Heidegger, 1996, p. 121).

What the self 'owns' is clear from Heidegger's central understanding of Dasein: it owns a capacity, a potentiality for being open to its own Being. But there is also a tendency to cut itself off from those aspects of human existence that are threatening, puzzling or uncontrollable. It is at this point that Dasein 'disperses' itself into the 'they', the 'one', the general with its denials and evasions. In that sense it loses what it owns.

Authenticity as an aim

Having questioned the generally accepted translation of Heidegger's 'Eigentlichkeit', I shall nevertheless – for reasons of wider communication but also because I have no more suitable word to offer – use the terms 'authenticity' and 'inauthenticity' in the following pages.

For Heidegger, both authenticity and inauthenticity are aspects of human being, are what he calls 'existentials'. We all have a capacity for authenticity, but are, in fact, 'lost' in inauthenticity most of the time. This 'dispersal into the They' is unavoidable, and Heidegger makes it quite clear that greater authenticity could not be reached by striving for it. In fact, he refuses to call it a 'better' state of being:

> We would also misunderstand the ontologico-existential structure of falling if we were to ascribe to it the sense of a bad and deplorable ontical property of which, perhaps, more advanced stages of human culture might be able to rid themselves. (Heidegger, 1962, p. 220)

The word 'falling' requires a comment. Heidegger did not, in fact, use the German word 'fallen', with its theological implications, but the word 'verfallen', which has the meaning of falling into the power of something from which we cannot escape. Stambaugh, translating 'verfallen' as 'falling prey', comes closer to this meaning than Macquarrie (Heidegger, 1996, p. 165).

Heidegger makes it clear that authenticity has nothing to do with genuineness. In a lecture which he delivered in 1927 and which became part of his *Basic Problems of Phenomenology* he says:

> This inauthentic self-understanding ... by no means signifies an ungenuine self-understanding. On the contrary, this everyday having of self within our factical, existent, passionate merging into things can surely be genuine, whereas all extravagant grubbing about in one's soul can be in the highest degree counterfeit ... Dasein's inauthentic understanding of itself via things is neither ungenuine or illusory as though what is understood by it is not the self but something else. (Heidegger, 1982, p. 160)

In another lecture included in *The Question of Truth* and given at the same time, Heidegger even more clearly denies that genuineness is an aspect of authenticity. This is mentioned in Michael Inwood's *A Heidegger Dictionary*, and as the English edition is said not to have appeared yet, I assume that the translation of the following sentence is his own:

> There is a false authenticity, i.e. a false case of Dasein's being-at-home-with-itself, and a genuine inauthenticity i.e. a genuine loss of itself, that arises from the concrete Dasein in question. (Inwood, 1999, p. 23)

These quotations show that it is a misunderstanding of Heidegger to interpret 'authenticity' as genuineness, and 'inauthenticity' as falseness.

A normative assessment of reality

If authenticity indicates what we really are, and inauthenticity a deviation into falseness, we introduce a normative assessment of what is real in existence that is quite alien to Heidegger's phenomenology. Heidegger does not offer a foundation for statements like: 'this is not the real me' or 'this is the person I really am'.

Alice Holzhey-Kunz, an eminent Swiss therapist and a 'Daseinsanalyst' but a critic of Medard Boss's way of using some of Heidegger's ideas, raises this issue:

> It is a misunderstanding to take authenticity as a norm and inauthenticity as a deviation from the norm. For authenticity appears then as an aim to strive for which is within reach, while inauthenticity is the fundamental possibility to lag behind this ideal and fail to reach it. (Holzhey-Kunz, 1992, p. 159 – my translation)

The introduction of a norm brings with it definitions of 'abnormality' and we shall return to the question of their relevance in the context of therapy. But our quotations have shown that one 'existential' is not more 'real' or 'normal' than another.

What is resolution?

We have seen that for Heidegger both authenticity and inauthenticity are dimensions of Being. Authenticity is the moment when Dasein confronts Being as it is, 'ready for anxiety' (Heidegger, 1962, p. 343), as it is anxiety that Dasein tries to avoid in its 'dispersal' into the generality of 'the they'.

At such a moment, Dasein is in a state of 'resolution'. 'Resolution signifies letting oneself be summoned out of one's lostness in the "they"' (ibid., p. 345). The word 'resolution' conjures up feelings of boldness, firmness and determination. The German word 'Entschlossenheit' has acquired similar meanings – but literally it means 'openness', the state of being 'unlocked'.

The following quotation shows clearly that Heidegger was not concerned with determination:

> The resoluteness intended in 'Being and Time' is not the deliberate action of a subject, but the opening-up of human being, out of its captivity in that which is, to openness of Being. (Heidegger, 1971, p. 67)

In the end we are left with Heidegger's crucial concern throughout his life – the question of human 'thereness' for the dimensions of Being.

Is the concept of authenticity relevant for therapy?

1. Alice Holzhey-Kunz continues her critique of Boss's interpretation of Heidegger's view of authenticity in the following way:

    > [Accepting authenticity as the norm] we are free, in a further step, to identify this norm of authentic existence – seen in a medical-psychiatric perspective – with health and maturity, and correspondingly to interpret inauthenticity, that is 'falling', as illness and deficient existential development. (Holzhey-Kunz, 1992, p. 159)

    It is her view that Boss, in fact, made this mistake. What is important to us here, however, is that she raises by her criticism the elusive question of the aim of psychotherapy. Has the concept of a 'norm' a place in it, and is it the therapist's aim to lead the client from a state of 'abnormality' to one that is considered closer to 'normality'? And even if we choose the less crude and more acceptable terms of 'maturity' and 'immaturity', are we not caught in the medical model, 'pathologizing' what we call psychological difficulties?

    We shall return to the question of the therapeutic aim. What we can say, at this point, is that the concept of an existential norm radically contradicts what Heidegger says about the dimensions of existence.
2. Originally the 'self' had no place within the theory of psychoanalysis which – with many variations and modifications – became the conceptual framework for most kinds of psychotherapy. Freud certainly did not use the concept. Since it has become part of the psychic configuration, its place has

been widely discussed, and particularly the difference from, or identity with, the 'ego' has become a focal point of this discussion.

In Great Britain the self was introduced in the Sixties by two psychoanalysts – D. W. Winnicott in his paper 'Ego Distortion in Terms of True and False Self' (1960), and R. D. Laing in his book *The Divided Self* (1959). Whatever the difference between the approaches of these two influential theorists – Winnicott was centrally concerned with child development while Laing tried to understand the schizoid personality – they revealed important common ground: both presented the self as 'divided' into a 'true' and a 'false' self. At first sight this assumption seems to show a striking similarity to Heidegger's distinction of an 'authentic' self and a 'they-self'.

It was Laing, deeply engaged as he was with existential ideas and the writers who explored them, who in a footnote related authenticity to his proposition of the divided self: 'The false self is one way of not being myself. The following are a few of the important studies within the existential tradition relevant to the understanding of the false self as one way of living inauthentically' (Laing, 1959, p. 94).

Laing then produces a short reading list which includes Heidegger's *Being and Time*, Sartre's *Being and Nothingness* and writings by Binswanger, to which he adds some psychoanalytic writings, among them Winnicott's *Collected Papers*.

Winnicott and Laing seem to share the assumption that there is a part of ourselves which tends to comply with the frequently hostile demands of the outside world – the 'false self' – while there is another part which refuses to do so – the 'true self'. Whatever form our compliance takes, it cuts us off from what we 'really' are. Thus the 'false' self prevents us from 'being ourselves', as Laing's footnote says, and makes us live 'inauthentically'.

The therapeutic task that arises from this assumption seems to be the dismantlement of the 'false' self so that the 'true' self, what we truly are, can emerge.

This would be essentially an 'intra-psychic' process. A 'divisible' self could only be part of 'the usual capsule-like representations', which in Heidegger's view had to be relinquished and to give way to a fundamentally different understanding (Heidegger, 1987, p. 3). Such understanding sees each of us as 'being-in-the-world', involved with and as Da-sein potentially open to all that is. This does, of course, say nothing about the value and efficacy of a therapy based on such an intra-psychic model, but it shows why it cannot have a place in an approach inspired by Heidegger's views.

My own problem with the use of 'true' and 'false' in therapy is that I cannot think of a criterion to distinguish the 'true' from the 'false' in a person, nor do I know who could make such a distinction.

It cannot be 'false' to live 'inauthentically', it cannot be more 'real' to live 'authentically', if both these states are aspects of existence itself. Accepting Heidegger's understanding of what has been translated as 'authenticity' it is as 'real' not to face Being (as we are most of the time) as to be open to it.

Heidegger's refusal to advocate a striving for greater 'authenticity', to see it as an advanced state of being to which we should aspire, does not, of course, mean that he does not regard it as an important possibility: he values it as a fundamental human capacity. But he refuses to see its absence either, theologically, as a state of sin, or, medically, as a state of illness. 'Authenticity', the facing of Being as it is, is one of the existential dimensions to which we respond one way or another.

3. Perhaps a comparison with what we, in a wider sense, call creativity might be helpful. Anxiety may make us turn away from the possibility of creating a painting, or a close relationship, and we may experience this turning away as a failure in the context of our life. Similarly a turning away from Being, a response not made, an answer not given may be experienced as a failure. This need not be so and there is

no inevitable link between past disengagement and present disturbance. Inauthenticity does not necessarily lead to suffering. But it may do so. And in this case there is a place for it in existential therapy.

We have seen that Heidegger asks therapists to avoid ontological interpretations of ontic events (Heidegger, 1987, p. 162). But we have also seen that ontic events contain 'pre-ontological' references to 'existentials'. Our avoidance of unacceptable aspects of Being is such a pre-ontological 'inclusion' which may be experienced ontically as one of the many forms of suffering. It seems to me that the client should not be prevented from this wider understanding of his/her suffering by the therapist. But it can only be the client who embarks on such a wider understanding. Otherwise disclosure may turn into exposure.

12 | Thrownness and Choice

What is thrownness?

It is often thought that one of the important aspects of existential thinking is the offer of the freedom to choose what we want to be. This is not necessarily welcome – Sartre says we are 'condemned' to it. It gives us a limitless responsibility for our life that is often experienced as a burden. Sartre seems, in fact, to put his emphasis on such a freedom. Heidegger, on the other hand, balances it with his description of our thrownness:

> Dasein is something that has been thrown; it has been brought into its 'there', but not of its own accord. As being, it has taken the definite form of a potentiality-for-Being, which belongs to itself and yet has not given itself to itself. As existent it never comes back behind its thrownness in such a way that it might first release this 'that-it-is-and-has-to-be' from its Being-its-Self and lead it to the 'there' (Heidegger, 1962, pp. 329-330)
>
> (I think Macquarrie is wrong in translating 'gehört' as 'heard' rather than 'belongs' and I have re-translated this sentence following Stambaugh.)

Heidegger emphasizes the limits to our freedom. We always already find ourselves in a situation, 'thrown' ontologically into the conditions of our existence (e.g. being mortal, being-in-the-world, being-with-others, being embodied) but also 'thrown' ontically into our particular history (e.g. social circumstances, relationships, culture, language).

Our thrownness is the unchosen basis on which our freedom to make choices rests:

> And how is Dasein this thrown basis? Only in that it projects itself upon possibilities into which it has been thrown. The Self, which as such has to lay the basis for itself, can *never* get that basis into its power; and yet, as existing, it must take over Being-a-basis . . . In being a basis – that is, in existing as thrown – Dasein constantly lags behind its possibilities. It is never existent *before* its basis, but only *from it* and *as this basis*. Thus 'Being-a-basis' means *never* to have power over one's ownmost Being from the ground up. (Ibid., p. 330; emphasis in original)

As I understand this difficult passage, Heidegger suggests that at any moment we are not able to choose just any possibilities but only those which are part of the basis of our total present situation. Every new situation offers new choices – what we are not free to choose is the basis itself. What is behind this basis, whatever led to its formation, is out of reach.

In other words, we cannot change the past, but as it becomes part of the present situation it opens up new possibilities of approaching it. This, in my view, is the point where change enters the orbit of therapy. We shall return to it.

Possibilities and choices

A great deal of psychotherapy is so determined by the traumatic origin of difficulties that it is often difficult to see possibilities of change. At first sight Heidegger's idea of 'thrownness' may seem to echo this. However, as a basis offering itself as a 'potentiality-for-being' it is, in fact, a springboard for the choice of new possibilities.

It is strange that Heidegger is so often presented as a philosopher of doom and despair. He is essentially engaged with possibility, with the future as an aspect, even as a source of the present. Persons seeking the help of a therapist frequently experience their situation as a trap where no choices are left. Heidegger's 'thrownness' is no trap but a fact, a present situation with its own possibilities. Possibilities may imply the presence of choices.

The moment of choice is the moment of 'resolution', and we need to remember the literal meaning of the German word 'Entschlossenheit' as a state of 'being unlocked'. Once again, the relevant characteristic is that of 'openness' – feeling trapped is, of course, a state of 'being locked in'.

What we choose is, as we have seen, limited to the possibilities which our present situation contains: 'The resolution is precisely the disclosive projection and determination of what is factically possible at the time' (ibid., p. 345). (The literal translation of what appears here as 'disclosive projection' would be 'unlocking intention'!)

Again, what *is* already and where we go from there is carefully balanced. Similarly, Heidegger reminds us that 'freedom, however, *is* only the choice of *one* possibility – that is, in tolerating one's not having chosen the others and one's not being able to choose them' (ibid., p. 331). This common source of confusion and irritation is close to everyone's actual experience.

To choose or not to choose?

If we have to choose between two possibilities, neither of which meets our wishes as fully as we would like, we feel that we can suspend choice. Phenomenologically, such a suspension is, in fact, impossible. By choosing not to choose we choose the situation as it is. In reality, we cannot avoid choice, but we can deceive ourselves into believing that we have not made a choice. However, our capacity to respond, our 'responsibility' is part of our existence – and it includes our capacity to respond in one way rather than another. Whatever our response is, it is a choice.

In the following passage, Heidegger focuses on a particular instance of our capacity to respond:

> To the call of conscience there corresponds a possible hearing. Our understanding of the appeal unveils itself as our *wanting to have a conscience*. But in this phenomenon lies that existentiell choosing which we seek – the choosing to choose a kind of Being-one's-Self which, in accordance with its existential structure we call *'resoluteness'*. (Ibid., p. 314; emphasis in original)

The special instance Heidegger addresses here is the choice of 'openness' which is also the choice of what has been (misleadingly) translated as the 'authentic' self, as we have seen. He introduces the call of conscience and the choice is between listening or not listening to this call. It is our fundamental concern for Being which makes us wish to listen to this call for openness, though our anxiety makes us turn away from it. Choice is clearly involved in either case.

Conscience and guilt

When Heidegger introduces 'conscience', he does not mean the 'public conscience' of which he says that it is nothing but 'the voice of the "they"'. He goes on to say:

> A 'world-conscience' is a dubious fabrication, and Dasein came to this only *because* conscience, in its basis and esssence, is *in each case mine* – not only in the sense that in each case the appeal is to one's ownmost potentiality-for-Being, but because the call comes from the entity which in each case I myself am. (Ibid., p. 323, emphasis in original)

In other words, this conscience is not concerned with reminding us of the rules of 'morality' which are ontic, but rather calls us to the realization of what our existence is essentially about – our openness to Being. As Dasein, in this area, 'constantly lags behind its possibilities' (ibid., p. 330), it always remains 'indebted' to Being. 'Indebtedness' is one of the meanings of the German word 'Schuld', and it is this 'existential' which Heidegger emphasizes in saying: 'Conscience is the call of care from the uncanniness of Being-in-the-world – the call which summons Dasein to its ownmost potentiality-for Being-guilty' (ibid., p. 323). Guilt as indebtedness is here the very core of being human.

Mineness

In our quotation introducing Heidegger's view of conscience we find the statement that 'conscience, in its basis and its essence, is *in each case mine* . . . the call (of conscience) comes from that entity which in each case I myself am' (ibid., p. 323).

This may surprise readers who are under the impression that Heidegger avoids any reference to the individual human being and has chosen the term 'Dasein' to take its place. However, Dasein is not a being, but a *way* of being – being *there*. Heidegger in his introductory remarks on 'Dasein' says in Joan Stambaugh's translation (which I prefer): 'The Being whose analysis our task is, is always we ourselves. The Being of this being is always mine' (Heidegger, 1996, p. 39).

And later he says:

> In accordance with the character of *always-being-my-own-being (Jemeinigkeit)*, when we speak of Da-sein we must always use the *personal* pronoun along with whatever we say: 'I am', 'You are'.
>
> Dasein is my own, to be always in this or that way. It has somehow always already decided in which way Da-sein is always my own. The being that is concerned in its Being about its Being is related to its being as its truest possibility. Da-sein *is* always its possibility ... And because Da-sein is always essentially its possibility, it can 'choose' itself in its Being, it can win itself, it can lose itself, or it can never and only 'apparently' win itself. (Ibid., p. 40)

(Note: Stambaugh's translation does not distinguish between the ontological Being (Sein) and the ontic being (Seiendes). I have changed her text by introducing the capital B for the ontological Being.)

In Heidegger's thinking the individual person is usually seen in a context – the context of others, the world, history and time. Heidegger's thinking is not centred in the individual. On the other hand, the individual is not swallowed up by a 'system' – there is a balance between 'mineness' and world, they constitute each other mutually. Though we cannot define the individual outside the world with others, it is the individual who responds to the world of which he is a part.

If the moment of resolution is also the moment of responsibility, it needs to be a moment for 'mineness', for saying 'I'. We have seen what happens when the distinction between individual responsibility and collective resoluteness disappears, as it did so stridently in Heidegger's delusion about Nazi openness to Being.

Therapeutic relevance

1. We have already seen that people seeking the help of therapy often experience their situation as a trap without a way out. Some may realize that they have contributed to the construction of this trap by making certain choices, but now they find themselves in a situation where no choices are left to them. Their only responses are helplessness and despair.

   Heidegger's view of 'thrownness' as a basis for the realization of new possibilities breaks the link between the uncontrollable fact and our response to it. An 'unlocked' response may lead to greater 'openness' and reveal so far unseen aspects of the fact. But even if this fact appears unchangeable, a new response may place it into a new context in which it acquires a new meaning.

   This creates a place for change within therapy that, in my

view, even the most meticulous reconstruction of the problem's origin does not offer.

2. A great deal of psychotherapy is determined by an exploration of past events. The past is crucial in Heidegger's thinking too – it is the very 'thrownness', the 'facticity' from which our possibilities arise. Within the orbit of our possibilities we make our choices. Our future is already there, so to speak, though as yet unrealized.

   It is in this area that our 'indebtedness', our guilt is located – but it is a guilt that is different from the one we usually meet in therapy: it is inevitable, 'existential', for 'we always lag behind our possibilities'. This guilt cannot be 'analysed', reduced or eliminated as if it were the one produced by what Heidegger calls 'public conscience'(which has some similarity to Freud's 'super-ego'). But this guilt can be confronted, responsibly and in openness.
3. Guilt as existential 'indebtedness' may be more meaningful and bearable than a blurred feeling of having failed in some obscure way. The acceptance of existence's lack of completeness, and the inevitable failure of an attempt to complete it by realizing all our possibilities, may open our understanding to aspects of Being we tend to avoid. Such understanding can lead to responsibility rather than to self-blame.

13 Heidegger's Understanding of Existence: An Overview

After considering various aspects of Heidegger's thinking and their potential relevance to psychotherapy, we need to look at the total context in which these aspects connect and whether this context does, in fact, offer the soil for the roots of an existential therapy.

We have seen that the total context within which Heidegger's thinking moves is the question of Being, or more precisely the meaning of Being. Being is the ground of everything that *is* in its particular way. For everything that *is* there is always the possibility of Non-Being.

The special position of human beings

Among beings only human beings have a concern for their Being, though they are often forgetful of it. They are also acquainted with the possibility of Non-being when they become aware of their mortality.

Heidegger singles out human beings for having this special capacity for knowing that they *are* as well as knowing *how* they are in their many individual ways. It is this potential awareness that differentiates them from other beings, and which Heidegger calls their 'existence'. Heidegger adopts the literal Latin meaning of the word, that is 'standing out'. Human beings 'stand out' sufficiently from *what* they are to be able to know *that* they are and that they might not be. Thus if we want to describe what the universal aspects of human being, the so-called 'existentials', are, we need to ask human beings.

Being-in-the-world

Heidegger opened his Swiss seminars with a statement that rejected 'all capsule-like representations . . . of a psyche, a subject, a person, an Ego, a consciousness' and suggested instead that 'the new ground of human existence should be called "Da-sein" [Being-there or Being-in-the-world]'. Here he is proposing a fundamental shift: the centre for an understanding of being human is no longer placed within individual consciousness but in a wider context of which we are a part. We may not have chosen to enter it in the first place, but we are free to choose to respond to it in one way or another. By being part of this context we also co-create it.

Ecological ideas on interconnectedness and the dangers inherent in splitting off or isolating parts of the whole have been accepted in various fields, particularly by natural science. What is less readily comprehended is the fact that a part cannot be properly understood unless we try also to understand as much as possible of the whole it belongs to. More concretely: the pebble on the table is not the same being as the pebble on the beach; the tiger in the cage is not the same being as the tiger in the jungle; the client in the consulting room is not the same being as the client at home. In other words in order to understand what we experience we must not 'bracket' the world, we need to understand it.

Being-with

Heidegger does not see the individual as a self-sufficient entity, entering the world more or less complete, though ready to be influenced by it. He presents the individual as a part of the world from the very beginning, in an interaction that makes the influence mutual. Thus human development is bound to some extent to be unpredictable, depending on an interplay within an ever-changing context. What remains unchanged is the fact of 'Being-with', that is our inevitable Being-with-others. We may respond to this in many different ways, but there is no departure into total isolation.

While human relationship is thus existentially given, it is our responses to this 'given' which shape the many forms our involvement with each other takes. Avoidance and denial of Being-with is one possible version of such a response.

Language as Being-with

For Heidegger, language is one aspect of existential relatedness. He sees language ontologically as the relation between address and response and the spoken word only as one ontic manifestation of it. There is always language, even if nothing is said.

Heidegger makes it clear that communication never ends, as it is essentially our dialogue with Being. Being addresses us continually and we respond in many different ways. Turning our back to what addresses us is one way.

Existence as body-mind

We have a powerful urge to take things apart in the hope that it will be easier to master them separately. However, though we think we are tackling a part, we always take on a whole the outlines of which escape our view. This means the collapse of an artificial dualism and the end of all final answers.

One dualism that disappears in Heidegger's approach is that of the separation of body and mind. Though Descartes's insistence on a complete separation of one from the other no longer predominates in our thinking, we still tend to perceive body and mind as separate entities, though most of us would admit to a more or less close interaction. This interaction is usually seen as causal, and the body is given some priority in that it is seen to generate 'mental' qualities in a way that remains obscure even to many neuroscientists.

Here is an opportunity to observe the difference between an explanatory approach and a phenomenological approach. There are clearly two different aspects of Being, one physical and another non-physical. Though they are always seen together – who of us has, in fact, met a mindless body (unless it was dead) or a bodyless mind? – they are always talked about as if they are separate entities. But in fact whatever happens to us, whatever we do, involves both aspects of our Being, the physical and the non-physical, and can be perceived as such. This is the phenomenological approach that is not concerned with stating or denying explanatory connections.

Existence's attunement

We have seen that Heidegger's existential 'Befindlichkeit' has been badly translated as 'state of mind' by Macquarrie, and more adequately as 'attunement' by other writers. Attunement manifests itself ontically as 'Stimmung', which has generally been rendered as 'mood'.

As I discussed earlier I propose to use the word 'feeling', instead of mood, which brings out more clearly what Heidegger, in my view, wishes to say about the affective aspect of human existence. What Heidegger seems to stress is that our 'feelings' are as much embedded in our context, in the situation in which we find ourselves and to which we contribute, as anything else we are and do. Feelings cannot be just understood as an element that can be added to or removed from what *is*. Our feelings, if understood in this way, do not survive the context to which they belong. Once more we have the collapse of a separation – the separation of 'feelings' from other 'mental' attributes like 'reason'.

Existential temporality

In his view of time, Heidegger brings together, once again, what is often considered apart. Past, present and future are different dimensions of time, but they do not follow each other as so many 'nows'. The past becomes an aspect of the present, and so does the future. The present is influenced by what has happened and also by what is anticipated. The experience of time is not linear but web-like.

For therapists who are concerned with the original insult that brought about the present injury, it is usually the past that is the most important temporal dimension. But for Heidegger it is the future that dominates because it is limited by our mortality. Heidegger views death as the end of our possibilities, since as human beings we are essentially the carriers of possibilities. Heidegger's concern with death is not a sign of an obsessive morbidity (as it is sometimes seen) but emphasizes our unique ability to make the possible real as long as we can do so.

The past, on the other hand, is for Heidegger what at times he calls our 'thrownness' or our 'facticity'. It is what is given and may in itself be beyond change, but is open to a possibility of change by a change in response. Again we have an interconnected flow of a variety of aspects which need to be understood rather than sorted out into a sequence of 'theres' and 'nows'.

The priority of phenomena

In his initial statement in Zollikon Heidegger described 'existence as "Dasein" as the opening up of a sphere where the sense of what is given can be perceived' (Heidegger, 1987, pp. 3–4). Existence is 'a sphere of potentiality of perception and awareness'. To speak of the 'perception and awareness' of 'what is given' is to speak of an openness to the phenomena themselves, as they are experienced in their immediacy, before they have been explained and categorized. It means giving the phenomena priority.

We have seen that it was Husserl who created the phenomenological approach. But we have also seen that for him the phenomenon to be explored was consciousness and that meant suspending whatever had no bearing on what consciousness essentially was. For Heidegger the phenomenon to be understood was existence and if existence was 'Being-in-the-world', the world could not be suspended.

It needs to be added that towards the end of his life – under the influence of Heidegger, as some writers think – Husserl introduced the concept of a 'Life-world' (Lebenswelt) into his considerations. But, as Pivčević points out, Husserl's 'Life-world' was not experienced by an actual person confronted with what is, but 'had to be explained in a priori transcendental terms, and that meant returning to the transcendental Ego . . . ' (Pivčević, 1970, p. 89). At this point, immediate experience, as Heidegger understood it, was left behind.

The important characteristics of phenomena, as Heidegger understood them, is that it is they themselves, not we, that offer their meanings, and that these meanings are never final.

Being and beings

All beings, non-human and human, have Being – that is, they *are*. All beings, non-human and human, are at any time in a particular way. A table, for instance, may be brown and covered with books. John, for instance, may be unhappy and study geography. *That* they are Heidegger calls their ontological aspect; *how* they are at a particular time he calls their ontic aspect.

But human beings, as we have seen, have a special kind of Being: they *exist*. They relate to their Being and have the capacity to care for it. Non-human beings, as Heidegger assumes, do not do so. (This, I feel, is a supposition on his part in the case of animals.)

Existence has some aspects that are potentially experienced by all human beings and these aspects Heidegger calls 'existentials'. Heidegger has not given a complete list of these, as far as

I know, but some of them recur frequently: Being-in-the-world, Being-with, embodiment, thrownness, temporality, language and mortality.

'Existentials' are given aspects of existence – we have not chosen them but are free to respond to them one way or another. 'Existentials' are ontological (aspects of Being). Our responses are ontic (our particular way of being). There may be friction between an existential and our response to it.

The question of authenticity

'Authenticity' is the generally accepted translation of Heidegger's word 'Eigentlichkeit', which he himself created by turning the adjective 'eigentlich' into a noun. (It is interesting that he does not use the word 'authentisch', which is part of the German language!)

I think that 'authenticity' is a bad translation because it conjures up the opposition between reality and falsehood, genuineness and fake, and as we have seen (in Chapter 11) this is not what Heidegger is talking about. 'Eigentlichkeit' is derived from 'eigen' (own) in the sense of 'uninfluenced by general opinion, the they'. Heidegger refers specifically to our capacity to confront Being with all its anxious dimensions instead of turning our back on it.

Heidegger does not advocate the 'owning' of Being as an aim but simply describes it as a capacity we have. He does not say that it is a capacity to strive for. However, he clearly thinks of it as an important capacity as it makes it possible for us to be the 'there' of Being. At the same time he stresses that it is inevitable that we can realize this possibility only rarely. 'Uneigentlichkeit' (inauthenticity) is also an aspect of existence.

Thrownness and choice

If human beings are carriers of possibility, they are necessarily capable of making choices. But their choice is limited by what is already given, their 'thrownness', their 'facticity', which includes their past. Also by choosing one thing, they leave another inevitably unchosen.

Making a choice is always an answer, a response to an address of Being in one of its various manifestations. We may be able to evade a particular choice, but we cannot avoid responsibility, as a denial of response is in itself a response.

Heidegger stresses that a choice is an answer to a call of conscience, and that this conscience is not a 'world-conscience', the voice of a general morality, but is '*in each case mine*', and that 'the appeal is to one's ownmost potentiality-for-Being' (Heidegger, 1962, p. 323). Heidegger talks about the choices we make in the area of our relation to Being, its possibilities and limitations.

We have seen that Heidegger does not see human beings as 'individuals', that in his view they are never complete in themselves, but involved in the world, fundamentally related to others. But where our relation to Being is concerned, the responsibility is 'mine'. When we speak of our relation to Being, 'we must always use the personal pronoun along with whatever we say: "I am", "You are"' (Heidegger, 1996, p. 40).

Heidegger's thinking is neither individualistic nor systemic. There is a careful balance between person and world. This balance he betrayed stridently and destructively in his alliance with the Nazis and his delusion that their thoughts had anything to do with his.

I must also admit that I have at times a feeling of unease about his later transformation of Being into some kind of divine authority, thus threatening our freedom of choice by what seems to be a call for obedience.

In *Being and Time* Heidegger leaves us in no doubt that evading a response to Being is as likely as, if not more likely than, a 'choosing to choose'. An answer to the address of Being means creating openness haunted by anxiety. But a refusal to answer may leave a feeling of 'indebtedness' (Schuld), which is one of the meanings of the German word for guilt. This is what has been called 'existential' guilt, and as we always 'lag behind our possibilities' such guilt is unavoidable.

14 Towards an Existential Therapy

TWO QUESTIONS ARISE when we consider Heidegger's thinking as the soil for the roots of a form of psychotherapy. Firstly, is it appropriate to base a therapy on a body of philosophical ideas? And then, is a specifically existential practice, in fact, possible?

Philosophy and therapy

Many people see philosophy as a separate discipline with its own choice of themes and its own language – rather abstract and difficult to follow. Above all, it seems to have little relevance to questions of everyday life.

This was, of course, not always so. It was certainly not so for Socrates, Plato or Aristotle. And there was no clear distinction between philosophy and science until well into the eighteenth century. Philosophical questions were, and for some philosophers still are, questions asked by human beings about their place in the world, their relation to other people and themselves. It is in exploring such questions that philosophers and therapists converge. In this sense therapy is always a philosophical enterprise, as it 'attends' to the experience of Being as such, as well as to the particular ways of being of persons who have chosen to seek some help in therapy.

Thus the distinction between, say, psychoanalysis and an existential therapy does not consist in the one having no 'philosophy' and the other being based on one. All therapy has a philosophical aspect in that it is concerned with the experience of the world, of others in the world, of ourselves in the world. The difference is in the fact that different therapies view this experience differently. All therapeutic views rely on the phenomena through which these experiences reveal themselves. Most kinds of therapy try to *explain* these phenomena. Existential therapy tries to *understand* them.

Explanation and understanding

Wilhelm Dilthey, a German philosopher whom Heidegger cited at some length in *Being and Time*, distinguished the natural and physical sciences from what he called 'Geisteswisssenschaften' (literally, sciences of the spirit, generally translated as the 'human sciences') by emphasizing the difference between 'explanation' (Erklärung) and 'understanding' (Verstehen). A lucid description of this difference is given by Rudolf A. Makkreel in *The Cambridge Dictionary of Philosophy*:

> The distinction between the natural and the human sciences is ... related to the methodological difference between explanation and understanding. The natural sciences seek causal explanations of nature – connecting the discrete representations of outer experience through hypothetical generalizations. The human sciences aim at an understanding (Verstehen) that articulates the typical structures of life given in lived experience. Finding lived experience to be inherently connected and meaningful, Dilthey opposed traditional atomistic and associationist psychologies and developed a descriptive psychology that Husserl recognized as anticipating phenomenological psychology. (Makkreel, 1995, p. 203)

We shall return to some of the issues raised in this description – that is, the difference between psychodynamic and existential interpretation (psychodynamic interpretation is explanatory whereas existential interpretation is hermeneutic). There is also a need ingrained in our culture to take the phenomena apart, 'atomize' them, in order to reconnect them into something that carries our meaning rather than theirs.

Is an existential practice possible?

But before we take a more detailed look at how an existential therapeutic practice flows from a Heideggerian view of the human experience of Being, we need to confront the question whether in fact such a practice is possible and what it would involve.

Many students of the writings of Heidegger, particularly those who are therapists, wonder whether his concepts, and perhaps any concepts of existential thinkers, can be brought to bear on therapeutic practice. Doubts may take the form of the question of how these ideas, difficult to grasp in themselves, can be 'applied' to the everyday work with suffering persons in which the therapist's task consists.

On the other hand, there are those therapists who believe that it is the very absence of rules and strategies, of what is called 'technique', which separates the existential approach from other therapies. They wonder how it would help if existential speculations took the place of psychoanalytic constructions.

Practice and technique

At this point I would like to suggest a distinction between practice and technique. If we believe, as psychoanalysts do, that in the world we live in the real meaning of what we experience lies hidden *behind* the phenomena, and that we cannot trust what meets the eye and reaches the ear, then we need to devise interpretative means to decipher the phenomena. This is not technique but practice – it flows from psychoanalytic beliefs.

If we believe, as existential therapists do, that we must allow the phenomena their own voice to tell us what they are, we need to sharpen our perception of what meets the eye and reaches the ear. There is nothing else to look for. This is also practice and not technique.

The practice is, so to speak, the other side of our beliefs. Practice is not the 'application' of ideas generated somewhere and passed on to somewhere else. Rather it is the enactment of our belief.

Technique arises when there is a gap between enactment and belief. We use technique when we have lost the connection with what we believe. This loss of connection may be the consequence of our practice having become mechanical, inflexible and routine. It may also be due to the fact that though our practice no longer reflects what we believe, we know it to be a convenient answer to a troubling question. Under the pressure of anxiety therapists slide from time to time into technique. It is the avoidance of that openness to the phenomena, which Heidegger sees as a denial of a very distinctly human capacity. It is inevitable but reversible.

Aspects of existential practice

From 'psyche' to 'with-world'

The first thing that needs to be understood is that an existential therapy cannot, in fact, be a 'psycho-therapy', if by 'psyche' we mean – as many therapists do – a hypothetical structure inside a person within which 'intra-psychic processes' are instrumental in bringing about a person's behaviour. If the context of our existence is the world, which always includes other people, it is this context in which what we experience as our inhibitions and disturbances occur. It is a change of this context, or a change in our response to it, that may help us with what we have come to call 'psychological difficulties'.

The place for therapy is thus not a 'psyche' within a person, and the aim is not a weakening or strengthening of the hypothetical components of such a psyche. The place for therapy is the wider context of which a person is part and co-creator, and the aim is an exploration of the response of this person to this context, leading to the question: to what extent is a change of this response desirable or possible?

Final explanation or unlimited understanding

What is the nature of the exploration of this context, and what do we perceive in it? What we perceive are the various phenomena of our relation to this context. This includes our relation to others and to ourselves and our relation to the 'givens' of this context, which, as we have seen, we have not chosen. These may be circumstantial, social or aspects of our personal history, or 'existentials', dimensions of Being itself like the presence of others, our anxiety and our mortality. The phenomena do not 'explain' anything, but their perception helps clients and therapists to 'understand' the situation that they are trying to explore.

This exploration does not assume that the 'real' meaning lies 'behind' what we meet, perceive and experience. It relies on the meaning that these phenomena reveal at the moment when we meet them. But this does not imply that the phenomena convey *all* they mean at this moment. On the contrary, any meaning points at further meanings, but meanings grow from each other, they do not replace each other. Total meaning will always be beyond our reach. There are no final answers. Existential interpretation is a step-by-step clarification where every answer poses a new question. In this kind of therapy, understanding grows but is never complete. Questions of diagnosis and prognosis can have no place in it.

The other: basic relatedness

As a dimension of the context that gives meaning to our existence, other people play a central part. We cannot understand ourselves in isolation from others. The 'with-world' is always a world we share with other people. There is a basic relatedness between human beings before we can talk about particular forms of relationship. This basic relatedness shows itself at one end of the spectrum in our mutual dependency and at the other end in our shared concern with Being as such.

How we shape this basic relatedness, how we deal with the actual relationships which are the ontic phenomena of our ontological relatedness, is inevitably an aspect of our existential exploration. There are many ways of realizing the possibilities of such relatedness just as there are many ways of denying them. Love and hatred can thus be understood as responses to existence itself rather than as projections and sublimations of biological impulses.

As we have seen, Heidegger has often been criticized for not having paid enough attention to individual relationships. But it has to be acknowledged that his thinking has given a firm ground to the fact of relatedness as such. As existing human beings we have the capacity to relate, it is never just 'missing', but we need to understand 'how' and whether we are willing to relate.

Therapy: a particular kind of relationship

We can already see what the therapeutic relationship is not. It is not the possibility of a therapist telling people in need of help how to understand their situation. A therapist cannot be an expert on other people's situations. The therapist has the task to enable persons in need of help to establish a place in which the understanding of their situation becomes possible.

We have seen how the understanding of a situation grows, not by narrowing down the target to a 'cause' or a cluster of causes, but by extending the range of questioning and broadening the area of discovery. Only the client can do this, assisted by the therapist. But therapists need to remember how easily their assistance can become coloured by their own suggestions.

The therapist is also no expert in deciphering phenomena – they are not symbols but say what they mean, though it may be difficult to understand what it is they mean. The therapist may however help clients to open up to phenomena without trying to decipher them.

It may seem as if the therapist has very little to offer – until we realize how rare it is in a relationship for one person to put him or herself entirely at the service of another, without giving in to the need to know and show it. There are few therapists who have not succumbed to this need at one time or another, particularly under the pressure of the client's attempts to extract from their therapists the very knowledge they cannot have.

As we can see even from this sketchy outline, the 'therapeutic relationship' is complex and many-sided but for all that no less genuine than other relationships. The therapeutic relationship is a phenomenon as much beyond final explanations as any other phenomenon.

Of course, previous experiences and anticipating wishes of a client are part of the present situation, as they are in any situation. But they are not 'transferred' from the client onto the therapist – they are a dimension of the existential fabric of the situation itself.

Language: a phenomenon of relatedness

Whatever the orientation of therapy language plays a central part. Heidegger sees language as an expression of the 'Being-with-ness' of human beings – communication is, in the widest sense, a dimension of Being. Though the spoken word is its most obvious instance, communication goes beyond verbal expression and in fact never ceases. Lack of communication is of course also a form of it.

In therapy, all phenomena 'speak' to us, as does the context in which the phenomena are perceived. We can pay too much attention to the actual 'text' at the expense of the context, as for example in the insistence on a 'verbatim transcript' of what is said. This is more likely to happen in an explanatory interpretation, which seeks for definite answers, than in a hermeneutic exploration, which takes each answer as a basis for a new question. The total situation is always more richly meaningful than any spoken words and its meaning is multi-dimensional and elusive.

Let us remember that Heidegger sees our relation to Being as essentially one of communication – Being addresses us and we respond.

Living time

What we frequently meet in our consideration of existential practice is the multi-dimensionality of existence – connections are not linear but web-like. This is also so in our experience of time, another important aspect for most types of therapy.

Existential phenomenology does not see time as a sequence of 'nows' but as three-dimensional. The past is always part of the present that contains an anticipation of the future. An exploration of a client's present difficulty does not stretch into the past in search of a determining 'cause' or cluster of causes, nor, for that matter, into the future in search of a determining wish or aim. Instead an existential therapist is involved in an exploration of whatever it is that makes up the client's present situation, and past and future will certainly be present dimensions. Above all, we will leave it to the client to connect whatever phenomena appear meaningful at the time in whatever way. Thus the client's difficulties will not be 'explained' but will be gradually, if not fully, understood.

Heidegger was troubled by the thought that we might think of ourselves as living 'within' time as if it was some kind of metaphorical space. He suggested that we were 'living time' where the past is the basis of a present which is the springboard for the realization of possibilities.

The body–mind dilemma

The most striking example of the separation of two aspects of existence, which can never be perceived apart, is the much debated body–mind dualism. Being human has two aspects – one physical, the other non-physical. But you will not find one without the other until death, when only the body is left, which then rapidly changes into something quite different.

There is a strange assumption that one must have in some

way generated the other, though as far as I know there is no satisfactory suggestion how this might be possible. When the mind's origin is considered, it is usually assumed that the brain has given rise to it. On the other hand, therapists are confronted with the notion that emotional distress turns magically, as it were, into physical symptoms.

The existential-phenomenological view proposes that all existing beings have a physical and non-physical dimension and that any disturbance affects the whole person. The degree of intensity with which the physical and non-physical aspects are affected may, of course, vary with the constellation of the situation in which the disturbance arose. But it seems probable that the physical and non-physical spheres are both involved simultaneously. What we call anger is both a physical and a non-physical state.

Divorced feelings

Another break-up of what is experienced as a whole, is the separation of feelings from the situation to which they belong. There is a belief that anger, sadness, love and so on when not expressed at the time are somehow 'stored' (for instance, in a place called the 'Unconscious') and can be revived later outside the original situation in which they arose. It is even thought that feelings can be attached to new situations.

But existential therapists see feelings as belonging to the situations in which they arise – they can be as little 'detached' from them as the pattern can be detached from the carpet. The anger of today is not the anger of years ago – whatever its relation to the earlier anger may be – it has a new context and is a different anger. The possibility of change depends on the realization that this is so.

Another consequence of such an isolation of feeling from situation is seeing a feeling as a transferable object rather than one dimension of an indivisible whole. This is an example of the separation of 'emotion' from 'reason', which is such a powerful assumption in Western thinking. Whereas, in fact, emotion and reason are as little met apart as body and mind. We have all encountered the powerful feelings that permeate the process of 'intellectualization'.

Choice: limits and possibilities

Psychotherapy has never found it easy to define its aim, whatever the orientation. But there is usually an idea of 'change' at the core of it. People invariably come into therapy searching for a change in a situation that has become difficult or intolerable. It is by the degree of change that the result of therapy is generally assessed.

But how does such a change come about? Do therapeutic explorations affect the situation itself in a way that makes it less difficult or more tolerable? Or is it a change in the response of clients that changes their experience?

If it is a change in the response that brings about a change in the experience we assume that clients have a choice to change their response. It is a belief of existential thinking that we have the freedom to change our response to situations, even when these situations appear to be or are in fact unalterable. Without a belief in such a freedom – which of course has been questioned – the notion of bringing about change seems difficult to sustain and therapy appears to lose direction. The choice *not* to change one's response is, of course, a choice too.

This freedom is in no way unlimited. Though there is a view within existential thinking that gives us complete freedom to choose how we live, this is not Heidegger's view. He carefully distinguishes what we are free to choose from what is 'given'. Whatever situation we are now in, whether originally chosen by us or not, may seem beyond change. Whenever we make a choice, we create a situation with new 'givens'. People who seek out therapy for help usually feel trapped by 'givens' that seem unchangeable.

It is at such a point that a space for freedom opens up. For our response is part of the context in which it was made and contexts do change. In therapy clients have the possibility to become aware of a new context for, say, a painful childhood memory – new because the past has now become part of a different present that includes a wealth of more recent experiences. This new context becomes clear as therapy offers clients an unusual opportunity to remember, articulate and freely connect whatever enters their awareness.

Whether the result is a change of response and thus a loosening of fixed connections will, of course, also depend on the client's choice. Whatever we choose involves our response-ability, our capacity to answer openly to what addresses us. It is this that Heidegger calls 'Eigentlichkeit', which has been misleadingly translated as 'authenticity'. Here the therapist's assistance ends. We need to remember how Heidegger has described 'Eigentlichkeit' (authenticity) in order not to turn it into an 'aim' to be 'achieved'.

Choosing existence

Before concluding this outline of an existential therapy inspired by the thinking of Heidegger, something remains to be said about those 'givens' that Heidegger called 'existentials'. They are aspects of existence itself and cannot be changed. We cannot live our life outside the world or isolated from other people, we cannot live without a body and we cannot live forever. We cannot avoid anxiety when faced with the possibility of *no* possibilities and we cannot choose the world into which we are thrown. But here too we have the freedom to respond one way or another. We can evade limiting and frightening aspects of existence in many different ways – by denying them, avoiding them, or distorting them by viewing them through the distorting lenses of addiction and compulsion.

Heidegger, though stressing the necessity of keeping what clients bring to therapy at the ontic level, also referred to a connection between 'existentials' and our everyday experience. He makes this very clear in his statement about the relation between anxiety and fear:

> ... only because anxiety is always a latent 'Being-in-the-world', can such 'Being-in- the-world' ... ever be afraid. Fear is anxiety, fallen into the 'world', inauthentic [uneigentlich], and as such, hidden from itself. (Heidegger, 1962, p. 234)

This appears to indicate an ontological meaning to the ontically varying spectrum of fears and phobias.

I would not suggest that it is the therapist's task to 'interpret' the ontological meaning of the various symptoms which people bring into therapy. But I have observed that clients will come across such meanings themselves and are helped by understanding them.

The denial of various unwelcome aspects of existence cannot, of course, be 'pathogenic' as such denial is itself an aspect of existence. But if the aim of therapy is greater understanding, if openness to phenomena is a singularly human capacity then an exploration of ontological relevance must be allowed a place in existential therapy.

However great Heidegger's reluctance may have been to tell us what to do, there can hardly be any doubt that he considered 'choosing existence' to be a choice of surpassing value.

A Personal Postscript

IN MY INTRODUCTION I described my need for a different framework for my work as a psychotherapist: the explanatory psychoanalytic model in which I had been trained did not sufficiently help me to understand the experience I had with my clients.

I related how it was in the writings of a group of Swiss therapists that such an alternative opened up. Their work was influenced by the thinking of the philosopher Martin Heidegger, and my own reading of a number of his writings confirmed my impression that his thoughts about the human position in the world reflected, in many ways, my own. I felt increasingly that many of Heidegger's thoughts offered an alternative soil for the roots of a therapy which derived its strength from his way of envisioning the phenomena of existence. In this book I have attempted to outline various aspects of this vision and to indicate their therapeutic relevance.

For me it was Heidegger's view of existence as 'Being-in-the-world' that most strikingly shifted my therapeutic perspective. The interconnectedness of all existential phenomena, what some people call Heidegger's 'holism' and George Pattison refers to as his 'deep ecology' (Pattison, 2000, p. 207), has led me to make a decisive therapeutic move. This is the move from the exploration of individual and necessarily fragmentary experiences to a clarification of an ever-growing (and, in fact, limitless) context where understanding takes the place of explanation. Throughout the book instances of the clarification of context and its therapeutic relevance can be found.

This priority of context within therapy is also the reason why – after serious consideration – I have decided not to illustrate my text with the usual excerpts from 'case histories'. Such illustrations are inevitably always 'out of context' and can be misleading within a form of therapy which aims at the understanding of as wide a context as possible. Particular therapeutic events, when separated from their context, can easily be misunderstood as exemplifying a number of 'typical' situations, though they belong, in fact, uniquely to the context in which they occur.

Finally, I would like to make a personal comment on Heidegger's 'basic question', which is the permanent theme of all his thinking, the question of Being.

We met it first in the form in which he put it at the end of his inaugural lecture at Freiburg University: 'Why are there beings at all, and why not rather nothing?' This was in 1929. In 1943 this lecture was republished with a postscript which contains the sentence: 'of all beings, only the human being, called upon by the voice of being, experiences the wonder of all wonders: *that* beings *are*' (Heidegger, 1998, p. 234).

This sentence expands and enriches the meaning of the original question. Only human beings have been entrusted, by 'the voice of being' itself, with the knowledge that 'beings *are*'. And more importantly, this fact is 'the wonder of all wonders'.

This sentence conveys to me a meaning of Being which is certainly implied by a great deal of what Heidegger has said about it, but rarely quite so clearly, and, I may say, so enthusiastically, as here. Namely that Being is something extraordinary, to be treasured and cared for by human beings who alone among beings know about it.

What is it that makes Being so extraordinary? Heidegger does not really tell us. What he does is to imply in his original question that anything that *is* might also *not be*. This does not tell us why we should treasure Being, all we have been told is that forgetfulness of Being is a 'privation' or a 'deficiency'.

This is how far Heidegger takes us until, at a later point, he transforms Being into a kind of divine power that demands us to be 'there' for it. Then care turns into obedience. Whatever others may feel about this, I am unable to follow along this road and it certainly leaves the area of therapy.

As existential therapists we need perhaps to make our own choices about the ways in which we relate to Being, keeping, however, within Heidegger's orbit in realizing our special position as existing human beings. As such, we alone are able to remember Being, and are therefore also able to forget it. To which I wish to add our ability to destroy it.

To me the passionate tone of the sentence from the 'postscript' asks us to acknowledge, even be grateful, that beings *are* – not only human beings, not only living beings, but also inanimate beings that have only Being and no existence.

I am reminded of the fact that the German version of 'there is' is 'es gibt', which means 'there is given'. That beings are given to us, Heidegger sees as 'the wonder of all wonders', a 'gift', so to speak, that cannot be taken for granted, that asks us for engagement and response. As far as I know, Heidegger does not express this so distinctly and unequivocally, but it seems to me that his view of the various aspects of existence points in this direction.

In any case, Heidegger made it clear at the end of his life that he wished he could call the publication of his writings 'ways' rather than 'works'. My own way of understanding the human relation to Being as engagement and response has helped me to see that our difficulties are often not so much the result of conflicts 'within' ourselves, but are a reluctance or refusal to accept those aspects of Being, which can be as frightening and painful as they are real.

References

Caputo, J. D. (1993) *Demythologizing Heidegger*. Bloomington: Indiana University Press.

Cohn, H. W. (1997a) *Existential Thought and Therapeutic Practice*. London: Sage.

Cohn, H. W. (1997b) 'Heidegger and the Jewish Existential Psychotherapist', *Journal of the Society for Existential Analysis*, 8(2): 95–9.

Condrau, G. (1998) *Daseinsanalyse*. 2nd revised edn. Dettelbach: J. H. Roll.

Cottingham, J. (1993) *A Descartes Dictionary*. Oxford: Blackwell.

Damasio, A. R. (1994) *Descartes' Error: Emotion, Reason and the Human Brain*. London: Macmillan.

Dostal, R. J. (1993) 'Time and Phenomenology in Husserl and Heidegger', in C. B. Guignon (ed.) *The Cambridge Companion to Heidegger*. Cambridge: Cambridge University Press.

Farias, V. (1989) *Heidegger and Nazism*. J. Margolis and T. Rockmore (eds). Philadelphia: Temple University Press.

Freud, S. (1909) *Notes upon a Case of Obsessional Neurosis*. Standard Edition (S. E.) Vol. I. London: Hogarth Press.

Freud, S. (1916) *Introductory Lectures on Psycho-Analysis*. S. E. Vol. XV. London: Hogarth Press.

Freud, S. (1917) *Introductory Lectures on Psycho-Analysis*. S. E. Vol. XVI. London: Hogarth Press.

Frie, R. (1999) 'Interpreting a Misinterpretation: Ludwig Binswanger and Martin Heidegger', *Journal of the British Society of Phenomenology*, 30 (3): 244 ff.

Heidegger, M. (1962) *Being and Time*. Trans. J. Macquarrie and E. Robinson. Oxford: Blackwell.

Heidegger, M. (1971) *Poetry, Language, Thought*. Trans. A. Hofstadter. New York: Harper and Row.

Heidegger, M. (1982) *The Basic Problem of Phenomenology*. Trans A. Hofstadter. Bloomington: Indiana University Press.

Heidegger, M. (1985) *History of the Concept of Time*. Trans. T. Kisiel. Bloomington: Indiana University Press.

Heidegger, M. (1987) *Zollikoner Seminare* Protokolle-Gespräche-Briefe. Ed. M. Boss. Frankfurt-am-Main: Klostermann. (My own translation.)

Heidegger, M. (1993) 'What is Metaphysics?' In D. F. Krell (ed.) *Basic Writings* (revised edn). London: Routledge.

Heidegger, M. (1996) *Being and Time*. Trans. J. Stambaugh. Albany: State University of New York Press.

Heidegger, M. (1998) Postscript to 'What is Metaphysics?' Trans. W. McNeil, in *Pathmarks*. Cambridge: Cambridge University Press.

Holzhey-Kunz, A. (1992) 'Psychotherapie und Philosophie', *Daseinsanalyse* 9, pp. 153–62.

Husserl, E. (1991) *On the Phenomenology of Internal Time Consciousness*. Trans. J. Brough. Vol. 4 *Collected Works*. The Hague: Nijhoff.

Inwood, M. (1999) *A Heidegger Dictionary*. Oxford: Blackwell.

Laing, R. D. (1959) *The Divided Self*. Harmondsworth: Penguin Books.

Makkreel, R. (1995) *The Cambridge Dictionary of Philosophy*. Ed. R. Audi. Cambridge: Cambridge University Press.

Mautner, T. (ed.) (1996) *Dictionary of Philosophy*. Harmondsworth: Penguin Books.

Merleau-Ponty, M. (1962) *The Phenomenology of Perception*. Trans. C. Smith. London: Routledge and Kegan Paul.

Moran, D. (2000) *Introduction to Phenomenology*. London: Routledge.

Olafson, F. (1998) *Heidegger and the Ground of Ethics*. Cambridge: Cambridge University Press.

Ott, H. (1994) *Martin Heidegger: a Political Life*. Trans. A. Blunden. London: Fontana Press.

Pattison, G. (2000) *The Later Heidegger*. London: Routledge.

Petzet, H. W. (1993) *Encounters and Dialogues with Heidegger 1927–1976*. Trans. P. Emad and K. Maly. Chicago: University of Chicago Press.

Pivčević, E. (1970) *Husserl and Phenomenology*. London: Hutchinson University Library.

Polt, R. (1999) *Heidegger: an Introduction*. London: University College London Press.

Safranski, R. (1999) *Martin Heidegger: Between Good and Evil*. Cambridge Massachusetts: Harvard University Press.

Sartre, J.-P. (1958) *Being and Nothingness*. Trans. H. Barnes. London: Methuen.

Solomon, R. S. (1987) *From Hegel to Existentialism*. Oxford: Oxford University Press.

Spinelli, E. (1989) *The Interpreted World. An Introduction to Phenomenological Psychology*. London: Sage Publications.

Steiner, G. (1992) *Heidegger*. 2nd edn. London: Fontana Press.

Winnicott, D. W. (1960) 'Ego Distortion in Terms of True and False Self', in *The Maturational Processes and The Facilitating Environment*. London: Hogarth Press.

Wolin, R. (ed.) (1993) *The Heidegger Controversy. A Critical Reader*. London: MIT Press.

Recommended Reading

Binswanger, L. (1963) *Being-in-the-World. Selected Papers*. Trans. J. Needleman. New York: Basic Books.

Boss, M. (1979) *Existential Foundations of Medicine and Psychology*. Trans. S. Conway and A. Cleaves. Northvale, New Jersey: Jason Aronson.

Cohn, H. W. (1997) *Existential Thought and Therapeutic Practice*. London: Sage.

Cooper, D. E. (1999) *Existentialism. A Reconstruction*. 2nd edn. Oxford: Blackwell.

Deurzen-Smith, E. van (1996) *Everyday Mysteries. Existential Dimensions of Psychotherapy*. London: Routledge.

Heidegger, M. (1962) *Being and Time*. Trans. J. Macquarrie and E. Robinson. Oxford: Blackwell.

Heidegger, M. (1993) *Basic Writings*. Ed. D. F. Krell. Revised edn. London: Routledge.

Heidegger, M. (1987) *Zollikoner Seminare* Protokolle-Gespräche-Briefe. Ed. M. Boss. Frankfurt-am-Main: Klostermann.

Pattison, G. (2000) *The Later Heidegger*. London: Routledge.

Polt, R. (1999) *Heidegger: An Introduction*. London: University College London Press.

Spinelli, E. (1994) *Demystifying Therapy*. London: Constable.

Index

Lightning Source UK Ltd.
Milton Keynes UK
UKOW030012030412

190032UK00001B/135/A